African American Presbyterian Clergywomen

This resource was developed in partnership with the African American Clergy Women's Caucus and made possible, in part, by a subsidy provided by Women's Ministry, National Ministries Division, Presbyterian Church (U.S.A.). Additional names and information were provided by the Office of the General Assembly, Presbyterian Church (U.S.A.).

In putting together this book, we have attempted to locate each person whose story is part of the evolving history of African American Clergywomen in the Presbyterian Church (U.S.A.). We regret that we were not able to be completely successful in this endeavor. We have also made every effort to verify and provide complete and accurate information about each person whose name is listed and apologize if there are any errors.

African American Presbyterian Clergywomen:

The First Twenty-Five Years

Compiled by
the Reverend Karen V. Brown
and the Reverend Phyllis M. Felton

Witherspoon Press
Louisville, Kentucky

© 2001 Witherspoon Press, Presbyterian Church (U.S.A.), Louisville, KY

Unless otherwise noted, Scripture quotations are from the New Revised Standard Version of the Bible, copyright © 1989 by the Division of Christian Education of the National Council of the Churches of Christ in the U.S.A. Used by permission. In some instances text has been slightly adapted to make the language inclusive.

Every effort has been made to trace copyrights on the materials included in this book. If any copyrighted material has nevertheless been included without permission and due acknowledgment, proper credit will beinserted in future printings after notice has been received.

Edited by Cassandra D. Williams

Book interior and cover design by Cecilia Amorocho Hickerson

First edition

Published by Witherspoon Press, a Ministry of the General Assembly Council, Congregational Ministries Publishing, Presbyterian Church (U.S.A.), Louisville, Kentucky

Web site address: http://www.pcusa.org/cmp

PRINTED IN THE UNITED STATES OF AMERICA

01 02 03 04 05 06 07 08 09 10 — 10 9 8 7 6 5 4 3 2 1

African American Presbyterian clergywomen: the first twenty-five years / compiled by Karen V. Brown and Phyllis M. Felton.—1st ed.
    p. cm.
    ISBN 1-57153-020-7
    1. African American Presbyterians—History—20th Century. 2. African American women clergy—History—20th century. 3. Presbyterian Church (U.S.A.)—Clergy—History—20th century. I. Brown, Karen V. II. Felton, Phyllis M.
BX8946.A35 B57 2001
285'. 1'092396073—dc21

00-069326

Contents

Acknowledgments

In 1974, the ordination of Katie Geneva Cannon to the ministry of Word and Sacrament catapulted the Presbyterian Church out of the slavery of sexism into the age of liberation.

This chronicle of us—the women, our story and our ministries—is in celebration and honor of this historic event. The contributions of the ordained African American clergywomen in proclaiming the gospel of Jesus Christ as preachers, educators, evangelists, professors, organizers, healers, directors, and administrators is evident throughout this publication.

Special thanks are extended to the Rev. Barbara Dua and Women's Ministries, PC(USA) for their financial support. We'd also like to thank the Rev. Curtis A. Jones, chair of the National Black Presbyterian Caucus, Curtis A. Kearns, Jr., the director of National Ministries Division, PC(USA), and the Rev. Rita L. Dixon and the Office of Congregational Enhancement, National Ministries Division, for their support and endorsement during this project. We also thank the staff of Congregational Ministries Publishing for their patience and tireless efforts in producing this twenty-fifth anniversary publication.

We dedicate this book to our "sheros" who paved the way and to all young African American girls who have heard God's call and are ready to follow, "Here am I, [Lord], send me" (Isa. 6:8).

Introduction

I WAS ABOUT SIX YEARS OLD sitting in church listening to my best friend's father preach. I remember thinking that maybe one day I would be a preacher just like him. However, I quickly dismissed this thought as I began to think of all the things little girls didn't do. Throughout my young life God's Spirit continued to tap me on the shoulder and I continued to argue with the Divine that I didn't know any African American Presbyterian women preachers. I had plenty of models of strong black women elders, but none who represented the possibility that I could say *yes* to this call of God on my life.

But on April 23, 1974, with no major fanfare, no special services, in the middle of a regularly scheduled Presbytery of Catawba meeting, the Divine declared to all, "This is my daughter, with whom I am well pleased." Katie Geneva Cannon had the courage to turn a deaf ear to the negativity within the world and the church and to listen to the call of God on her life. As we celebrate twenty-five years of African American clergywomen in the Presbyterian Church (U.S.A.), we have grown from one to twelve to seventy-five. Saying *yes* to God can start a revolution.

African American Presbyterian Clergywomen seeks to share with you a glimpse of the precious jewels of African descent who continue to give of themselves in the ministry of this church. Behind every name, ordination date, ministry site, sermonic reflection, meditation, and prayer is the story of a sister empowered by the Holy Spirit to do the work of God.

Our gifts have not been readily welcomed or received. Too often we have been judged by a harsher standard than our male counterparts. Too often we have been stepped over for less qualified candidates. Too often the gifts we have brought to the church have been thrown back in our face. But the words of the Reverend Jimmie Hawkins to his sister the Reverend Annie Vanessa Hawkins, speak to all of us:

> You are facing a quadruple jeopardy in that you are female living in a male-dominated society; an African American female in a society that puts women on the bottom of the pay scale; a Presbyterian female seeking ordination in a denomination that ordains females, but does not necessarily push to place those females in the parish; and an African American Presbyterian female in a denomination that is struggling to be inclusive of all races in the midst of diversity. Realize our obstacles and stand firm in your faith.

And we have stood firm! The Reverend Opal Smith and the Reverend Ernestine Blackmon Cole both write in their sermonic reflections of the woman who dared to bring her expensive gifts to Jesus in the face of opposition and rejection by those who claimed to follow the Anointed One. The Reverend Doris Glaspy writes of the compulsion that we have to proclaim this great gospel! And the Reverend Rose Niles McCrary writes of "colored women preachers still climbing Leah's ladder unwanted and unloved but fertile as all the fragrant valleys that cradle civilization and life." Yes, we have answered the call and we have clung to the faith that brought our ancestors through.

Like a people of the diaspora we find our ministries throughout the United States and the world. From South Carolina to California, from Mount Vernon to Madagascar, from Baltimore to Brazil, from Cleveland to the Congo, from Georgia to Ghana, from Louisville to Washington, D.C., we have been instruments of God's presence and power. We cannot be boxed in to one aspect of ministry, because our very calls demand that we break through any box in which we are placed. Our ministries bear a variety of fruit. We are visionaries and preachers, we are healers and teachers, we are planners and builders, we are organizers and warriors. We are ministers of the living God telling the story of the Resurrected Christ in word, sacrament, and action.

I praise God for the Reverend Dr. Katie Geneva Cannon and all my sisters in ministry. God is to be praised for the congregations, communities, churches, and countries that have been transformed because God saw fit to create *African American Presbyterian Clergywomen* for such a time as this. I praise God for all who will come after us and gain strength from our stories.

African American Presbyterian Clergywomen is an invitation to celebrate the gifts of God at work in us. It is an invitation to join the journey that began twenty-five years ago with one sister saying *yes* to God and daring to represent what we all can be in the eyes of God. It is an invitation to hear God responding with "This is my daughter with whom I am well pleased."

The Reverend Robina M. Winbush

A Brief History

AFRICAN AMERICAN CLERGYWOMEN in the Presbyterian Church (U.S.A.) have been working since 1974 to establish supportive community, to engage in continuing theological education, and to explore the challenges of Christian ministry that are unique to us. Beginning in 1979, we recognized the urgent need to gather annually with other women of color who were ordained as Ministers of the Word and Sacrament in the former UPCUSA and PCUS. In powerful dialogues between the present and future, we wrestled with an unalterable set of facts that focused on the reunion of the denomination, the relocation of national offices, the impact of spiraling inflation that made severe inroads on restructured General Assembly agencies, downsized executive staff in synods and presbyteries, reduced programmatic mission budgets, leaving little flexibility for undertaking the new initiatives demanded by the Presbyterian constituencies whom we, as racial ethnic clergywomen, were called to serve.

Over the years, we traveled to meetings in Houston; San Francisco; Philadelphia; Kansas City; Stony Point, New York; Cairo, Egypt; and San Juan, Puerto Rico. Our major aim was to strategize regarding employment opportunities and special placement services, to resist white supremist conservatism and misogynist patriarchal exclusivity within our denomination, to advocate for bilingual education and bodily integrity, to expose unwritten rules of polity, and to increase our understanding of church administration and fiscal interdependence. Another desideratum was to make visible our curious invisibility. We published sermons, essays, poetry, reviews, a calendar of events, job openings, and usable truth in our monthly newsletter *Que Pasa*.

In a 1982 essay, the Reverend Ida Wells gave voice to the overall views and values, the concerns and commitments of the Racial/Ethnic Clergywomen's Conference. She spoke for many when she wrote:

> We, the women of the Racial/Ethnic Clergywomen's Conference, believe that we are created in the image of God, called according to God's purpose, and empowered to be God's instruments of love, peace, and justice in a troubled world. . . . We assemble for our own shelter, nurture, and spiritual fellowship so that we might participate more fully in the proclamation of the Gospel for the salvation of our sisters and brothers, in the maintenance of the divine worship in our churches, in the preservation of the truth of God, in the promotion of social righteousness, in the various Presbyterian communities to which we serve and to whom we return, with the assurance that the Holy Spirit has been at work in our midst.

More recently, a concern for the defunct Racial/Ethnic Clergywomen's Conference prompted the Reverend Karen Brown to call for an envisioning-organizing meeting of the African American Clergy Women (AACW) of the Presbyterian Church (U.S.A.) in Winston-Salem, North Carolina, on March 17, 1998. As might be expected, creating a Christian advocacy group, specifically for ordained women of African descent, generated numerous responses from clergy and laity alike. While opinions were strong and differences evident, the communication with the Clergy Women's Organizing Council was cordial throughout the next year.

At the gala 1999 celebration of the twenty-fifth anniversary of the ordination of African American clergywomen in St. Louis, Missouri, April 19–24, in conjunction with the Thirty-second Annual Meeting of the National Black Presbyterian Caucus, the official bylaws of AACW were approved. Although the structure, details, and constituency vary from the 1980 Racial/Ethnic Clergywomen's Conference, there was a high degree of enthusiasm from all participants as we worked to breathe life into this new body that will serve as an institutional nexus for the broad range of issues and activities concerning our ministries. This intergenerational, supportive network will address the antiliberationist backlash and the encroachment of racist sexism that clergywomen are currently experiencing. We will deal with the continuing conflicts and challenges faced by African American women in ministry, especially how we balance our personal and professional lives.

African American clergywomen in the Presbyterian Church (U.S.A.) are very grateful for the labor of love actualized by members of the Clergy Women's Organizing Council, Karen V. Brown, Bernice Warren, Diane Givens-Moffett, Rose Niles McCrary, Gloria J. Tate, Robina M. Winbush, Phyllis M. Felton, and Arlene W. Gordon. The African American Clergy Women's Caucus gives us a head start in a legitimate, supportive, and effective organization worthy of the highest degree of justice-making solidarity, as we enter the twenty-first century.

The Reverend Katie Geneva Cannon, Ph.D.

African American Presbyterian Clergywomen

The Reverend Katie Geneva Cannon, Ph.D.
Ordination Date: April 23, 1974
Ministry: Associate Professor of Religion, College of
    Arts and Sciences
Ministry Site: Temple University, Philadelphia,
    Pennsylvania

The Reverend Elenora Giddings Ivory
Ordination Date: September 5, 1976
Ministry: Director, Washington Office
Ministry Site: Washington Office of the Presbyterian
    Church (U.S.A.), Washington, D.C.
Scripture That Informs My Call: Amos 5:14–15

The Reverend Joan M. Martin, Ph.D.
Ordination Date: October 10, 1976
Ministry: William R. Rankin Associate Professor of
    Christian Social Ethics
Ministry Site: Episcopal Divinity School, Cambridge,
    Massachusetts

The Reverend Devia Pellam Phinisee
Ordination Date: November 1, 1976
Ministry: Pastor
Ministry Site: St. Luke Presbyterian Church,
    Dallas, Texas
Scripture That Informs My Call: (Exod. 2:8–14;
    2:23–25)

The Reverend Gloria J. Tate, D. Min.
Ordination Date: June 3, 1977
Ministry: Pastor
Ministry Site: Teaneck Presbyterian Church,
    Teaneck, New Jersey

The Reverend Rita L. Dixon, Ed.D.
Ordination Date: June 4, 1978
Ministry: Associate for Black Congregational
    Enhancement
Ministry Site: National Ministries Division,
    Presbyterian Church (U.S.A.), Louisville, Kentucky

The Reverend Marsha Snulligan Haney, Ph.D
Ordination Date: December 10, 1978
Ministry: Professor of Missiology and Religions of the
    World
Ministry Site: The Interdenominational Theological
    Center, Atlanta, Georgia

The Reverend Amitiyah Elayne Hyman
Ordination Date: February 3, 1980
Ministry: Director of SpiritWorks, Interim Pastor,
   Church of the Redeemer
Ministry Site: Washington, D.C.

The Reverend Portia Turner Williamson
Ordination Date: June 26, 1980
Ministry: Minister-at-Large
Ministry Site: New Hope Presbytery, Rocky Mount,
   North Carolina
Scripture That Informs My Call: Ps. 27:1a; Isa.
   58:6–9; Mark 16:9–10

The Reverend Morrisine Flennaugh Mutshi
Ordination Date: September 14, 1980
Ministry: Served as chairperson of the New
   Testament Department and Vice-Rector,
   Presbyterian University Sheppards and Lapsley,
   with the Presbyterian Church of Congo
Ministry Site: Charleston-Atlantic Presbytery

The Reverend Phyllis M. Felton, D.Min.
Ordination Date: December 14, 1980
Ministry: Pastor
Ministry Site: Valley View Presbyterian Church,
   Pittsburgh, Pennsylvania
Scripture That Informs My Call: Phil. 1:3–6

The Reverend Frances Camille Williams-Neal, D.Min.
Ordination Date: August 9, 1981
Ministry: Associate for the Hawkins Buchanan Fund
    for Racial Justice
Ministry Site: National Ministries Division
    Presbyterian Church (U.S.A.), Louisville, Kentucky
Scripture That Informs My Call: Matt. 7:7, Prov. 3:5–6

The Reverend Bernadine Grant McRipley
Ordination Date: October 18, 1981
Ministry: Associate, Domestic Issues
Ministry Site: Washington Office of the Presbyterian
    Church (U.S.A.), Washington, D.C.

The Reverend Brenda D. Brooks
Ordination Date: June 26, 1983
Ministry: Associate for Social and Racial Justice
Ministry Site: The Synod of the Trinity, Camp Hill,
    Pennsylvania

The Reverend Venetta D. Baker
Ordination Date: March 2, 1984
Ministry: Chaplain
Ministry Site: Western Carolina Center, Morganton,
    North Carolina
Scripture That Informs My Call: 2 Cor. 4:7–9, 2 Cor. 5:7

The Reverend Barbara B. Ndovie
Ordination Date: June 17, 1984
Ministry: Interim Associalte,
    First Presbyterian Church
Ministry Site: Ann Arbor, Michigan

The Reverend Willie M. Brazil
Ordination Date: June 26, 1984
Ministry: Pastor
Ministry Site: Saint Paul Presbyterian Church,
    Louisburg, North Carolina

The Reverend Toby Gillespie-Mobley
Ordination Date: May 1985
Ministry: Co-Pastor
Ministry Site: Glenville New Life Community
    Church, Cleveland, Ohio

Delrio Ligons-Berry, D.Min.
Ordination Date: September 11, 1985
Ministry: Minister-at-Large
Ministry Site: King of Prussia, Pennsylvania

The Reverend Wanda M. Lundy
Ordination Date: March 29, 1987
Ministry: Pastor
Ministry Site: First Presbyterian Church, Edgewater,
New Jersey

The Reverend Louwanda Harris
Ordination Date: July 12, 1987
Ministry: Associate
Ministry Site: Grace Memorial Presbyterian Church,
Pittsburgh, Pennsylvania
Scripture That Informs My Call: Luke 4:18

The Reverend Diane Givens-Moffett
Ordination Date: November 7, 1987
Ministry: Associate Pastor
Ministry Site: Elmwood United Presbyterian Church,
East Orange, New Jersey

The Reverend Brenda H. Tapia
Ordination Date: March 20, 1988
Ministry: Assistant Chaplain at Davidson College and
Director of Davidson College's Love of Learning
Program; Parish Associate, C. N. Jenkins Memorial
Presbyterian Church, Charlotte, North Carolina
Ministry Site: Davidson College, Davidson, North
Carolina; Charlotte, North Carolina
Scripture That Informs My Call: Matt. 6:33

The Reverend Sandra K. Edwards
Ordination Date: November 11, 1988
Ministry: Director, African American Ministries
    Program
Ministry Site: McCormick Theological Seminary,
    Chicago, Illinois

The Reverend Diane Corrothers Smalley
Ordination Date: December 11, 1988
Ministry: Campus Minister and Women of Promise
    Development Officer
Ministry Site: Eastern Michigan University, College
    of Health and Human Services, Ypsilanti,
    Michigan

The Reverend Robina M. Winbush
Ordination Date: January 8, 1989
Ministry: Director, Ecumenical and Agency
    Relationships
Ministry Site: Office of the General Assembly,
    Presbyerian Church (U.S.A.), Louisville, Kentucky
Scripture That Informs My Call: Isa. 65:17–25; Luke
    13:10–17

The Reverend Patsy Nichols Redwood
Ordination Date: February 26, 1989
Ministry: Minister of Christian Education
Ministry Site: St. Paul's Presbyterian Church, Los
    Angeles, California
Scripture That Informs My Call: Prov. 3:5–6

The Reverend Dr. Mary Ruth Newbern-Williams
Ordination Date: June 18, 1989
Ministry: Associate Executive Presbyter for Outreach
Ministry Site: Sheppards and Lapley Presbytery,
    Birmingham, Alabama

The Reverend Jacqueline E. Taylor
Ordination Date: October 26, 1989
Ministry: Associate Executive Presbyter
Ministry Site: New Castle Presbytery, Newark,
    Delaware

The Reverend Marinda Harris
Ordination Date: November 5, 1989
Ministry: Pastor
Ministry Site: Westhills Presbyterian Church,
    Atlanta, Georgia

The Reverend Opal Gurlivious Smith
Ordination Date: May 20, 1990
Ministry: Interim Associate Executive Presbyter and
    Staff Coordinator
Ministry Site: Maumee Valley Presbytery,
    Findlay, Ohiio
Scripture That Informs My Call: Luke 7:36–50; 8:1–3

The Reverend Ernestine Blackmon Cole
Ordination Date: April 28, 1991
Ministry: Associate Dean of Students
Ministry Site: Columbia Theological Seminary,
   Decatur, Georgia

The Reverend Arlene W. Gordon, D.Min.
Ordination Date: June 21, 1991
Ministry: Interim Executive Presbyter
Ministry Site: Detroit Presbytery, Detroit, Michigan

The Reverend Rose Eileen Niles McCrary
Ordination Date: October 27, 1991
Ministry: Pastor
Ministry Site: First Presbyterian Church, Mt. Vernon,
   New York

The Reverend Sylvia J. Wilson
Ordination Date: November 13, 1991
Ministry: Presbyterian Church (U.S.A.) Site
   Coordinator, Young Adult Volunteers and
   Coordinator for Visiotrs' Mission Experience
Ministry Site: Nairobi, Kenya
Scripture That Informs My Call: Gal. 5:1

The Reverend Rhoda C. Nixon
Ordination Date: December 15, 1991
Ministry: Parish Associate
Ministry Site: Sargent Memorial Presbyterian
    Church, Washington, D.C.

The Reverend Sylvia T. Walker
Ordination Date: June 13, 1993
Ministry: Pastor
Ministry Site: Westminster Presbyterian Church in
    Cedar Manor, Jamaica, New York
Scripture That Informs My Call: Psalm 103

The Reverend Doris Glaspy
Ordination Date: November 23, 1993
Ministry: Pastor
Ministry Site: Roseville United Presbyterian Church,
    Newark, New Jersey
Scripture That Informs My Call: Eph. 3:7–10

The Reverend Gwendolyn Deloris Magby
Ordination Date: 1994; acknowledged by
    Presbyterian Church (U.S.A.) in June 1996
Ministry: Assistant Minister/Youth Pastor
Ministry Site: St. Andrew's Chapel, Jonesboro,
    Georgia

The Reverend Karen V. Brown
Ordination Date: August 31, 1994
Ministry: Associate Pastor, Executive Director of the
  Lillie A. Ross Family Life Center
Ministry Site: Madison Avenue Presbyterian Church,
  Baltimore, Maryland

The Reverend Paula Owens Parker
Ordination Date: September 11, 1994
Minstry: Director, The Daughters of Zelophehad,
  Inc.,Spiritual Director, Richmond Hill
Ministry Site: Richmond, Virginia
Scripture That Informs My Call: Isa. 61:1–3

The Reverend Ethelyn R. Taylor
Ordination Date: October 31, 1994
Ministry: Pastor
Ministry Site: Oxford Presbyterian Church,
  Philadelphia, Pennsylvania

The Reverend Rhashell D. Hunter
Ordination Date: February 12, 1995
Ministry: Pastor
Ministry Site: Community Presbyterian Church,
  Flint, Michigan

The Reverend Angela B. Archer
Ordination Date: April 14, 1996
Ministry: Pastor
Ministry Site: North Shore Presbyterian Church,
    Great Neck, New York

The Reverend Eleanor Moody-Shepherd
Ordination Date: October 13, 1996
Ministry: Parish Associate, Chaplain, Director of
    Supervised Ministry and Coordinator for
    Certificate Program in Christian Ministry
Ministry Sites: New York Theological Seminary, New
    York, New York; First Presbyterian Church, Mount
    Vernon, New York; Open Arms Homeless Shelter
    for Men, White Plains, New York

The Reverend Belinda M. Curry
Ordination Date: June 1, 1997
Ministry: Associate, Policy Development and
    Interpretation, Advisory Committee on Social
    Witness Policy
Ministry Site: General Assembly Council,
    Presbyterian Church (U.S.A.), Louisville, Kentucky

The Reverend Annie Vanessa Hawkins
Ordination Date: March 22, 1998
Ministry: Mission Volunteer International,
    Lecturer/Volunteer, College of the Transfiguration
Ministry Site: Grahamstown, South Africa
Scripture That Informs My Call: Ps. 100:3,
    Rom. 12:1–2

The Reverend Stephany D. Graham
Ordination Date: May 16, 1998
Ministry: Associate for African American Leadership
Training and Resource Development
Ministry Site: Congregational Ministries Division,
Presbyterian Church (U.S.A.), Louisville, Kentucky

The Reverend Catherine M. Hughes
Ordination Date: August 23, 1998
Ministry: Stated Supply, First Presbyterian Church of
Los Angeles
Ministry Site: Los Angeles, California
Scripture That Informs My Call: Phil. 4:13

The Reverend Meri-Li Douglas
Ordination Date: October 10, 1998
Ministry: Member-at-Large
Ministry Site: Chapel Hill, North Carolina

Reflections

POSTHUMOUS EMBRACE

Calling your name
  my mouth feels bound.
Screaming out my love
  speech is snatched away.
You knew me once
  spoke fondly to me.
Unordained pain comforts me now.
Death's rock-hewn door
  flung wide-open,
Smearing the threshold
  with the blood of my soul.

I fell—
  accosted,
    cramped,
      terrified
through the crevice of the earth
  only to see
    a dreamlike apparition,
      a mere shadow
        of your former self.

Through special dispensation,
  I re-entered this realm.
Your fleshy clay
  remains beneath the ground.

Turning your back to ashes and dust
    as I gather you up
        in memories
            meshed in my dreams.

—*The Reverend Katie Geneva Cannon*

GOD WILL FIX IT

FROM THE EARLIEST OF TIME, people have been pondering over the circumstances and events of time. Certainly times are changing, and still there are a vast number of people who do not believe that there is a supernatural power called God who will fix everything according to their needs, if they would trust and obey God.

We find in the Exodus account that the experiences of God's people in Egypt teach many truths about God. One of the most delightful traits of God is God's providence. God took care of Israel from beginning to end.

Jacob's family came to Egypt to escape a famine in the land of Canaan. They were reunited with Joseph, the son of Jacob who had been sold by his brothers. Pharaoh gave Joseph's family the land of Goshen as a place of permanent residence.

For several years Joseph's family prospered and multiplied. After Joseph's death, another pharaoh, who did not know Joseph, came to power. This pharaoh was threatened by the Israelites, so he directed them to hard labor. The good life turned to disappointment and sadness, as it does for so many of us.

God had shown God's providence in past years. The Israelites had experienced the marvelous care of God. Now during the cruel experience of an arrogant king, God displayed Godself as the God who would ultimately take care and fix things for God's people. By the same token, God will ultimately fix things for the African American race in spite of the rampant racism and injustices that continue to plague us in America.

To declare that "God will fix it" is simply a way of declaring that God almighty will bring freedom, justice, and salvation to God's people.

The providence of God prevails over those who trust and depend on God completely.

What are some of the insights about the providence of God?

First, God's providence endures time. The story of Israel's bondage in Egypt demonstrates that God works in God's time. God did not deliver them with the first cry of bondage. Israel wanted immediate action, but God worked on God's own time schedule.

Second, God's providence withstands assaults. During times of assault, the enemy seems stronger than God. To the Israelites, Pharaoh's strength seemed stronger than Jehovah's might. Further investigation into God's providence demonstrates that God is stronger than the enemy. The entire Exodus story demonstrates the superiority of God over any power. Two Hebrew midwives expressed their faith in God's power: Shiphrah and Puah refused to obey Pharaoh's order to kill male Hebrew babies while the mother was in the birth process. These women saw a king greater than Pharaoh. Their faith was rooted in God's supremacy.

Deborah (the judge), Esther, Harriet Tubman, Sojourner Truth, and other women of faith during the biblical and slavery eras did not get dismayed over the state of their lives and the lives of their people. They believed in the superiority of God over any foe or power. These sisters of faith trusted in God for strength and deliverance.

God wants to come into your life so that you can experience God's unseen powers at work. Let God fix it for you!

The Reverend Devia Pellam Phinisee

TELLING THE STORY: OUR HERITAGE IN AFRICA

ONE OF THE MAJOR ISSUES that permeates all of our program, leader, and resource development for African American congregations, is our identity with Africa. Our congregations must develop a strong consciousness of our African heritage and relationship with other African people. This is absolutely crucial for a healthy relationship with God, self, and neighbor. It is also necessary for our liberation as African people. We must continue to be God's voice against racism, exploitation, and other forms of oppression in America, Africa, and the world. We have a special call to advocate for justice for Africa in public policy and the religious world.

I have traveled in Africa to Egypt, Ghana, Kenya, and Ethiopia. Our heritage in all these countries is extremely rich. The most recent journey to Ethiopia revealed Queen Sheba's palace, ancient huge stone monuments more than six feet high. All created ten thousand years before Jesus was born. We also explored huge stone churches carved out of mountains during the eighth century. We were filled with awe! How did they do this without the benefit of modern technology? We have a strong ancient African Christian witness in Lalibela, one of Ethiopia's holy lands. This prayer was inspired during the visit:

Holy God, Mother and Father of All Creation,
Thank You for This Visible Witness of You:

expressing yourself in stone,
creating and shaping cultures and civilizations,
correcting the human story,
making your truth known,
erasing the imprints of low esteem from African people everywhere.

Healing the wounds and freeing the spirit of forgiveness
that we all may be one with you and one another
making our joy complete.

With you in us and we in you,
we see your beauty in the curving hills and flowing valleys of
Lalibela,
a land where the Holy Spirit created churches out of stone.
We see your love in the swift nimble movement of gentle people
with large brown eyes

and in the travelers with bags, cameras, water bottles, calculators,
compassion and passion.

We feel your presence in the worshiping, greeting, resting, and
eating,
shopping, walking, and struggling, and
we are filled with your serenity.

The Reverend Rita L. Dixon

COMMUNION TIME

ANY PLACE WHERE WE ARE ABLE to pause and commune with God becomes our prayer closet. I've noticed lately that my carport has frequently served as my prayer closet at the end of a busy day at work. It has become a place of meditation as I mentally prepare to switch gears from the seminary community as a place of faith and learning, to my home as a place of family nurture and love. How I do appreciate those precious moments just to sit and be still!

What do I think about? Anything and everything. Recently two lighthearted, but thought-provoking questions have stayed on my mind. While attending a church conference a few days ago, a newfound friend remarked that she would have truly preferred having been born in another time and place in history. That started me wondering about what period of history I preferred living in—the past, present, or future? And a similar question asked in a different setting had to do with which biblical character I most identified with. I found the latter question surprisingly easy to answer; she is called Eve—the first woman who walked, talked, reflected, questioned, laughed, and discovered life with her Creator!

These questions, perhaps for me are so sensitive and deeply felt because I am lifting up in prayer two seminary colleague friends who are dealing with the tragic death of loved ones—one through suicide and the other (two family members!) by a freakish accident. Another couple I mourn with have lost a child who had not yet joined the world of the living. Several young people are having a difficult time as they attempt to "find themselves" in the tormenting teenage years of their lives. And I know several sister friends and family members who have health challenges and who are struggling to take care of themselves and others.

Regardless of how painful and chaotic these days might appear, without a doubt, I am a woman of the present—a woman of today. I know we are here because we stand on the shoulders of women and men, youth and children who have suffered and struggled before us. Therefore, we have an obligation to God, and to them, to use with wisdom the days, gifts, talents, skills, and minds that are given us. As Jesus reminds us in his teachings, his vision, and by his life, we must live wisely to build a just and hopeful future for the reign of God, both seen and unseen.

I don't envy those yet unborn or the youth of today. Unless we who are living (and especially those of the Christian faith community) are more faithful in fulfilling our destiny, we may realize only when it is too late that we have "majored in the minors, and minored in the majors."

Because of the current cultural winds of materialism, selfishness, and instant gratification we have often refused to authentically struggle and wrestle with some relevant ethical issues that affect us locally, nationally, and internationally; and as a result, our children's children will find themselves burdened not only with the newly emerging issues of their day, but also with the issues we have neglected and simply ignored.

Each time I teach seminarians, and speak or preach in congregations or church conferences, I become so keenly aware of the challenges we face in a society that does not encourage struggle, but rather convenience and expediency. We cannot give in to the temptation for easy living, but must boldly enter into a dialogue of action and reflection with those who seek liberation and transformation. We must partner with those who are shaping a better future.

Often I'll discover that thirty minutes have passed, and I'm still sitting in my car! Though I haven't solved the problems of the world, I am grateful for this prayer and the fact that God is God.

The Reverend Marsha Snulligan Haney

CREATION'S PRAYER

Great Spirit, Holy, High, and Lifted up,
We greet you this glad morning.
We welcome you into this place and call you forth.
In the silence we greet you in behalf of all people—

> Tree people,
> Plant people,
> Rock people,
> Insect people,
> Winged people,
> Finned people,
> Four-legged people,
> And two-legged people,
> Red, black, yellow, and white people.

You who shine light upon our path.
Who give us the moon, the sun, and the stars.
You who blow breezes to cool our hot burning.
You who send rain showers,
To quench our split and cracking dryness.
We greet you this glad morning;
Great Spirit, Holy, High, and Lifted up.

IMANI VILLAGE

Now faith is the substance of things hoped for, the evidence of things
    not seen.

(Heb. 11:1)

I
In the clearing stands a once-proud tree, adorned
With withered bodies of the lynched ones never mourned.

We gather in the clearing to do that mourning now.
To sing and shout our anguish, let their spirits bow.
We gather in the clearing, long lost and yet unborn
Ancestors, living dead, griot, dancers of the dawn.

Ours is a village, city-centered
with houses brick and gritty.
Muggings and shootings overhang our streets
Withering souls still embodied.

Come and go with me, I fear to go alone,
The journey is together into this danger zone.

Robust and hardy ones, believing as we go
A power goes before us who seeks out high and low.

We follow not by eyesight, hindsight, or foresight.
We follow by faith in the unseen seer
Who knows the cracks and crevices, the fences and the fears
That keep our village hostage to the suffering of years.

Once forbidden to read, now we do not care
Who hurts for the sneakers, and the chains we wear.
Gold replaced the iron ones clinging to our necks.
An overseer's lash more gentle than our guns
Pointed at each other while bullets burst in homes.
And laid upon the sidewalks are our progeny—
Young, gifted, black, and dead.

Come and go with me, I feel you hanging back
Our together journey cannot avoid this track.

II
Come and go with me to a place we've never been before,
Where auction block and slaver's ship can't hurt us anymore.
A place that's full of sunlight, where the drums again are played,
while grandmothers and grandfathers
See that which they've prayed.

Come and go with me. I cannot go alone.
The journey is together beyond this danger zone.

Weary tears and silent years so piteously spent
Give way not to laughter, feasting, a happening event.

We gather in here huddling close from island and vast stretch
Plantation, ghetto homelands, migrations north and west.
Riding freedom's buses and underground railway routes
Corporate ladders downsized tell us "Harvest your first fruits."

A nation built upon a rock long centuries ago,
Our rocksoil one, tear-watered, is ready now for planting.
The seeds of the faith can sprout here tendered by our hands,
And sorrow is tilled to shouting by full-throated bands.
With drums, and hums, and moans, the raps and the groans
Of a people coming home.

Come and go with me, the pace is picking up.
Nguzo Saba principles are posted above the deck
On the ship that sails the waters near our village.

The passengers are boarding—Marcus and Sojourner,
Harriet, Henry Highland, Frederick and Nat Turner.
Malcom's progeny and Martin's too. Ida B's and Mary Mc's
Queen Latifah and Nzinga are all now coming back.

"Harambee, Harambee, Harambee," let us shout
to browns and blacks, and reds and ruddies here and all about.
Come and go with me, come on, ya'll do come.
We're burning sage and singing, listening for the drum.

Star will light our way.
Rail will cleanse our path.
Sea will burst through forest.
Moon and heavens laugh.

Come and go with me, beyond the danger zone.
the journey is together, I cannot go alone.

Benediction
God bless you,
with a knowledge of the cost paid for your freedom.
God keep you,
nurtured and nourished in a family of faith that tells you
who you are and whose you are.

God cause a divine face to shine upon you, to be gracious
unto you, giving you what is needful and what is good for the living
      of your lives.
And God give you peace, with an appetite for justice.
An intolerance of mediocrity.
And a refusal ever to return to captivity.
God give you peace.
Amen.

The Reverend Amitiyah Elaine Hyman

A PROVERB OF THE CONGO

Bukalenge Bua Nzambi Ntshinsanga Nsanga Butu, Buimpe Mukulu Mukuate, Muakunyi Mukuate.

(The power of the church is sustained when people, adults, and children pray together).

THIS PROVERB IS A LIVING REALITY here in the Democratic Republic of the Congo, not only in the church but in daily life. In a land where democracy is not yet fully achieved and where poverty, disease, and death are daily companions, the people sustain each other through prayer, hospitality, and a genuine joy for being alive. It is a great joy and privilege for me to be in the ministry of God's church among such a people.

The Reverend Morrisine Flennaugh Mutshi

WORDS FOR MY SURVIVAL

The secret to possessing Joy is Resistance.

The Reverend Dr. Phyllis M. Felton

GOD'S CONSISTENT LOVE

I WORK AS A CHAPLAIN in a facility for people who have developmental disabilities and/or mental retardation. Significant developmental disabilities and mental retardation used to be called birth defects.

Working with this population has brought the passage regarding "earthen vessels" (2 Cor. 4:7) to life. We all have some irregularities, be it significant blindness or a bad hairdo. Even when your human frailties are most visible, and God should have given up on us a long time ago, God is always present and still has life and love to give us.

On beautiful autumn days, I am reminded that God's beauty, which is so prevalent in the fall leaves, is not just for the strong, rich, or powerful; it is for us all. While I may not be as capable as others of appreciating the colors of the leaves, I know that they are there. I know that the fall is present because of the apples, the cool mornings, and all the rustling underfoot. Bring on the pumpkins and hay bales!

I believe that God has a place where such things as beauty, strength, courage, wisdom, faith, and love are stored. If human beings could get their hands on them, these wonderful attributes would be packaged up and sold as our capitalistic world does. God knows how human beings can be and keeps these spiritual qualities out of reach. As we pray and use up the love that has been given to us, we receive more. When we make use of the courage that we have, God provides us with more; likewise, when we deplete the joy that God gave us, we find ourselves with more joy.

This is why we as Christians are hopeful people. We know that as long as we have life, God provides more life and living for us. We may be struck down, but we are never destroyed.

The Reverend Venetta D. Baker

A REFLECTION OF WORSHIP AND PRAISE IN ETHIOPIA

MY TRAVEL GROUP WAS GREETED at the airport in Lalibela by church members and honored during spirit-filled Orthodox services attended by the village people and led by the church leaders. In the days that followed as I experienced the joyous Maskal festival in Addis Ababa, the praise-filled youth service and the Sunday worship with the Ethiopian Evangelical Mekane Church Yesus, the Sisters of Charity, the International Evangelical Churches, and the children in the Mother Teresa House, I was humbled and awed as I witnessed firsthand the tremendous faith of the Ethiopian people. In spite of troubles of many kinds, like hunger, homelessness, joblessness, and illnesses of many forms, their faith is not destroyed and they praise God with joy and great energy.

By Jesus' very example, the Ethiopian churches know and express praise as an essential element in faith. When the people of God turn our focus away from ourselves and our lives, we enter God's presence in a very dramatic way. In the various worship experiences, I witnessed people from all social and economic levels coming to worship and praise, women and men, boys and girls, actively participating in and leading worship. Each seemed to come ready to offer up to God a sacrifice of praise, in spite of heartbreaking difficulties and troubles in their personal lives and in the broader life of Ethiopia, with a confidence that they are not, and shall not, be destroyed. As they beat the drums with power and play the keyboards and guitars, each stroke, each harmonious moan seems to cry out to God: "O God, we will hope and praise you more and more!" They know God has not deserted them or Ethiopia. Their praise and worship reveals one of the things that makes worship in the African and African American traditions so unique: we give a large space just to praising the Lord. It is simply being ourselves and letting in the Holy Spirit. Africans and Africans from the diaspora know that God has brought us too far not to praise God. We know that if we have breath in our bodies, if blood is flowing through our veins, if we are able to move about and have our being, we ought to just praise Almighty God.

The joyful praise and worship of the people of Ethiopia reveal that they are rich in faith and love for God. This is a great gift to offer, not only to God, but also to the rest of humanity.

The Reverend Toby Gillespie-Mobley

TO GOD BE THE GLORY

IN 1991, I BECAME THE FIRST woman pastor to serve the historic Lombard Central Presbyterian Church in Philadelphia, Pennsylvania. While there, I cofounded and directed the John B. Reeve Institute, a continuing education extension program of Howard University Divinity School. In 1997–1998, I was resident scholar at the Institute for Ecumenical and Cultural Research, where I wrote a biography of the Rev. Dr. John Bunyan Reeve.

My motto is: *All that I am or ever hope to be, I owe it all to God. To God be the glory.*

The Reverend Delrio Ligons-Berry, D.Min.

MINISTRIES OF OUTREACH

I WAS RAISED in the Bidwell Street Presbyterian Church in Pittsburgh, Pennsylvania. In 1966, I made a commitment to Christ and became a missionary-at-large of Pittsburgh Presbytery.

Early in my ministry, I founded and became director of the Glen House Mission, which was located in the Glenhazel Housing Project. In 1971 Glen House moved into the Hazelwood Presbyterian Church at 247 Johnston Avenue in Pittsburgh. In 1978, I was commissioned by the Pittsburgh Presbytery as a lay preacher. In 1981, I decided to attend seminary as a part-time student and in 1987 was ordained a Minister of the Word and Sacrament. I became the pastor of the Hazelwood Presbyterian Church, which was a mission field of Pittsburgh Presbytery. This mission operated a food pantry, a used-clothing store, and an enhancement program that offered tutoring in reading and writing skills. I also provided a Street Crusade and preached at the jail.

The Reverend Louwanda Harris

An African American Woman Reflects on Hong Kong and China

(McCormick Theological Seminary, Fall 1997)

CHINA IS MOVING TODAY from a state-owned and planned economy enterprise to a market economy. I found it interesting that you could buy land use for seventy to ninety years. However, you couldn't buy Chinese land because it was state owned. The handover brings a lot of feelings to the surface. Yet for me, my most enduring memory will be the young man who asked me at the Forbidden City where I was from. When I said Chicago, he told me I reminded him of the women he met in Botswana while he served two years in the armed forces.

The Reverend Sandra K. Edwards

CAMPUS COMMENTS: LOVE OF LEARNING MISSION

OUR KIDS ARE DROWNING.

Some sit in the back corner of their classroom and never participate in class discussions. Some curse, scream, or even strike out with their fists to defend themselves against these fires. Some have been wronged for so long that they forget what's right. And some wallow in self-pity, expecting handouts from hands that are much too cold. They use their sprinklers when they smell smoke; they continue to use them when the fire burns; and they forget to turn them off when the fire has been put out. And this is why they are drowning.

Davidson College's Love of Learning Program, directed by Assistant Chaplain Brenda H. Tapia, is an intense, holistic ministry that recognizes and helps young African Americans in Cabarrus, Charlotte-Mecklenburg, and Rowan-Salisbury School systems become better "world citizens" through education—a complete education. The goal of the program is to fully develop students intellectually, spiritually, and physically.

(It is all-accepting and teaches students not only who they are but whose they are.) Here you can be Presbyterian, Baptist, Muslim, or Buddhist and still be loved equally because religion isn't taught; it is practiced. It would be appropriate to include the words "Hate Need Not Apply" on the applications, because it is not tolerated. The program recognizes that as African Americans, the students are exposed to a vast amount of negativity. For the four weeks during the summer program, negativity is not allowed, and disrespect toward self or others is discontinued.

The Love of Learning Program has many missions. One important mission is that it teaches students to survive and thrive. At Love of Learning students learn that if they seek God first in all things, they learn how to stop drowning. As we continue to move forward in this new millennium into the chaos and turmoil that will inevitably persist, it becomes even more important that we remember our source of strength. The main reason any of us is here today and the major impetus for our ancestors' perseverance against insurmountable odds was that they knew to seek God first in all that they did. With all our education, we too forget the most basic lesson in life: that God is our source of supply, and that with God all things are possible. So, my brothers and sisters, if success in life still eludes you, or if you have gained the success you've been looking for and yet feel that something is missing, then take a few minutes (5 out of 1,440 in a day) to get still and listen to God. Work on your relationship with the Creator, discover who you are, why you are here, deepen your connection to the Divine, and discover the one and only true source of power on earth. Don't leave home without it.

The Reverend Brenda H. Tapia

JUST A SISTER AWAY: TAMAR'S TALE

(2 Samuel 13:10–19; Luke 8:40–42, 49–56)

THIS MORNING MARKS THE BEGINNING of Women's History month, and I have taken this opportunity to develop a series of sermons that address critical issues surrounding women in Scripture and in life. As you know, one of the things I love about Scripture is that it tells the whole story of humankind—the triumphant moments and the shameful moments in human history. It undresses our heroes and we see ourselves in the pain, the guilt, the challenges that our biblical heroes often face. Preachers are often very selective in choosing Scriptures. For generations we have overlooked those texts that we cannot easily redeem or we fail to tell the stories of the sometimes apparently superfluous characters. Historically, Scripture has been written, read, and interpreted from a male perspective. Even those of us who are women, seminary trained, and Spirit believing have often failed to look at some of the more difficult texts. However, the stories do not go away. The women of Scripture remain, waiting for us to hear their stories.

The title of this series comes from a book by the same title, *Just a Sister Away: A Womanist View of Women's Relationships in the Bible*, by the Reverend Dr. Renita J. Weems (Philadelphia: Innisfree Press, 1988). Dr. Weems is the first African American woman to receive a Ph.D. in Hebrew Scriptures, and she is a prolific writer. She writes for scholarly journals and for popular magazines such as *Essence*. The book *Just a Sister Away* gives attention to nine biblical stories involving women and their relationships with God, with one another, with the men in their lives, and with their children. This series is also indebted to the work of Dr. Phyllis Trible and her work *Texts of Terror: Literary-Feminist Readings of Biblical Narratives* (Minneapolis: Augsburg Fortress, 1984), which tells the stories of tragedy and terror in the lives of four biblical women.

This morning I covet your prayers about a woman named Tamar. This is Tamar's tale, but in truth it is the tale of so many girl children throughout history. It is the story of sisters who have grown old with the pain of a secret that has shaped their lives. It is the story of sisters who have suffered in silence and no one dared to tell their story. It is the story of families who have been torn apart from within. It is the story of families of every race, every nationality, religion, economic position, and social status. Tamar is just a sister away.

Tamar—daughter of King David, Princess of Judah, granddaughter of a Transjordian king (Tamar's mother had been given to King David in a politically arranged marriage). Tamar—a woman of beauty, wisdom, and grace. Tamar—a young woman who valued her body and her virginity. Tamar—a woman who respected the laws of God and of life. Tamar, with all her goodness and with all her father's power and prestige, could not be protected from the most basic of violations—the violation of her body.

Rape has often been used as a weapon of war. Whether we hear the horror stories of ethnic cleansing in Bosnia, or the rape of women in Rwanda, or the rape of women by troops throughout the world, whether we look at our own history in this country, our own family trees, or our own ancestors, some of whom were born to slave women raped by their masters and their master's sons, we know that rape is the expression of power and control. It is an expression of contempt and hatred. Without question, rape is a horror.

What happens when the violation comes not from a stranger, not from an enemy, not from the outside? What happens when rape comes from inside the family? Someone you know—someone who is supposed to protect you, someone whom you trust. What happens when rape and violation comes from someone who is supposed to love and protect you?

How many of you remember the book and the movie *The Color Purple*? When I first read the book in 1981, it took me a week to get through the first five pages. I could not stop crying, because I was working with young teenagers who were in foster care because they had been sexually abused within their families. I knew that what Alice Walker had written was not fictional, was not exaggerated, was not hype—it was Tamar's tale in a different time.

The facts of Tamar's story are clear. She had an older half-brother, Amnon. They shared the same father, King David, but had different mothers. Amnon was his father's firstborn son. He, like many young boys, had not been taught appropriately how to control his hormones. He had not learned appropriate boundaries. All he knew was that his sister was beautiful and he wanted to use her for his own sexual gratification. His cousin, Jonadab, helped him devise a scheme by which he would pretend he was sick. His father, King David, would come to ask him what was wrong and Amnon would request that his father send his sister Tamar to prepare a meal for him. Being the prince of Judah, being David's firstborn son and apparent heir to the throne, his request would not be denied. But Amnon's sickness was not to be cured with food. He did not want the food prepared by her hands; he wanted the fruit of her body. Tamar pleaded with him. Can you hear the pleas? "Please do not do this. You know this is wrong. This is evil. There is another way. Simply ask our father. *Please, big brother, don't! You will destroy me! Please don't! You won't be able to hold your head up high! Please don't!*"

And he raped her!

When he finished raping her, the story tells us that his lust turned to hatred. Often when stronger persons hurt weaker persons, they project their own self-hatred onto the other persons and hate them for being weak. Amnon kicks Tamar out of his room and locks the door behind her.

When she went into her brother's room, she wore the clothes of a princess virgin—a long robe with sleeves. When she came out, she tore her robe as a sign that she was no longer a virgin and could no longer be given in marriage. When she went in, she held her head high and she wore the beauty of her youth. When she came out, her head was hanging and she covered herself in the ashes of shame.

The real horror is not found in the rape. It is found in what happens after the rape. Tamar's brother, Absalom, found her and knew immediately what had happened. Absalom told her to keep quiet—after all, Amnon was her brother. The story tells us that Tamar remained in her brother Absalom's house, a desolate woman. When King David heard what happened, he was angry. But he failed to discipline Amnon because he "loved him" and he was his firstborn son.

I must confess that at this point in the story, I lose it. I do not understand what kind of parent would turn a deaf ear and a blind eye to his or her daughter's pain. What kind of parents would excuse their son for raping anybody's daughter, let alone their own daughter? What kind of parent believes that love means you never discipline, but allow your child to do anything he pleases to anybody he pleases? Maybe David couldn't discipline Amnon because he was consumed with his own guilt. For just a few years earlier, Amnon's father, King David, had raped another man's wife and had the man killed, so he could take her for his own wife. (The fruit doesn't fall far from the tree!) Maybe David couldn't discipline Amnon because he realized Amnon had learned from his daddy that he could do anything to anybody. Maybe David understood he was as much to blame as Amnon. For if everybody else knew Amnon was crazy about Tamar, surely the king knew. David had sent his virgin daughter into a situation where she was vulnerable and ultimately violated.

David's claim that his love for Amnon would not allow him to discipline him was foolishness. His temporary protection of Amnon cost him the lives of both his sons. David failed to discipline Amnon. When Absalom sees that his father will do nothing to vindicate the rape of his sister, he is filled with rage and plots to kill his own brother. That's the problem we see often in our families. We will identify someone as the "problem"—"the identified patient" as we call it in therapy. The one who comes is supposed to be the one who's sick. But the truth is that when tragedy hits anybody in the family, the whole family is in crisis. Absalom waited two years. For two years he comforts his sister and for two years he plans his attack on his brother. Then one day, while Amnon is partying and having a good time, Absalom comes and kills his brother. His father, having done nothing about his daughter's rape, is enraged, and Absalom is banished from the kingdom. Eventually Absalom plans a revolt to take the throne from his father. When King David's troops are protecting him, they kill Absalom. David lost both his sons because he failed to discipline one.

But David's failure to protect his daughter, his refusal to vindicate his daughter's pain, is beyond understanding. All he had to do according to the law was require Amnon to care for Tamar for the rest of her life and teach Amnon the lesson of confession and repentance. But David, king of Judah and Israel, David, the most powerful man in the country, David, who later mourns the death of his sons in the face of his daughter's pain, was silent. He did nothing.

What would have happened if David had called Tamar to him and pulled her close and said, "Baby, I'm sorry that this happened to you. I'm sorry that your brother violated you. But you're still my baby and I love you. I will let no one else hurt you. I will give you in marriage and you will be loved"? But David said nothing.

I suspect that the reason so many people suffer in silence, so many people suffer in pain, is because they are afraid of the response of those whom they love. They're afraid that people will point their finger at them and say, "You did something to deserve this." They're afraid that their families will turn on them and so they learn that it's better just to be silent and bear their pain alone.

I suspect something of Tamar died that day her brother violated her and her father did nothing. I suspect Tamar's self-esteem was destroyed beyond recognition. I suspect Tamar's ability to trust died that day. I suspect her own sense of sexuality became distorted. (One of the things I am learning about young girls who tend to be exceptionally promiscuous is if I listen attentively to their story, I will find and hear the story of their having been abused at a young age and their being totally confused about what is appropriate sexual behavior.) I suspect that Tamar's ability to be touched, to be genuinely loved, died that day. Her possibility of having meaningful relationships, of being held, of being touched, of knowing that she was special . . . I suspect it died that day. Scripture says that she lived as a desolate woman. Therapeutically, I can only guess that she battled depression and suicide for the rest of her life. Rape has a way of taking away more than your virginity or sexuality. Rape has a way of slowly killing an individual.

But I'm glad; praise God for Scripture. I'm glad David is not the only father in Scripture. I'm glad that through God's love and God's wisdom, God gave us an answer to Tamar's tale. When we turn to the eighth chapter of Luke, we find a man who was the leader in a synagogue. That meant he was a leader in the church, a man of position and power. But he also had a daughter, a little girl about twelve years old, and this little girl was sick unto death. And we are told that Jairus loved his daughter enough to risk his reputation, to risk his position, to risk his standing in the synagogue and the community. I suspect that Jairus would have given his very life, but he ran into the street and fell at the feet of an itinerant preacher named Jesus and begged him to come to his family's house. He begged him to heal his daughter. We may not know what this child's illness was, and we may not know what caused life to seep out of her body. We don't know how long she had been ill, but we do know that her father loved her enough to do something . . . to run and risk everything to get help for his baby girl. And I'm glad we have this story in Luke, because we see Jesus standing by the bedside of this dead little girl, and we can take all the little girls we know whose lives have been snatched from them, whose innocence has been stolen from them, whose virginity has been destroyed, and place them in the bed with that little girl. We hear Jesus saying to them, as he said to that little girl, "Child, get up!" And we are told she rose up from her bed just as though nothing had happened. Jesus restored life to that little girl and faith and hope to her parents. The family was touched by Jesus, for that which was dead came to life!

I am a living testimony that Jesus can come into your life and restore that which is dead. If you are a Tamar, or if you have a Tamar at home, if you meet Tamar on the street, if you know Tamar in your family, tell her that even if everybody else is silent and ignores her pain, there is One who sees her, there is One who loves her, there is One who wants to restore to her all that has been taken from her. His name is Jesus. And he will do what her brother didn't do, he will do what her mama and daddy didn't do, he will do what the social worker can't do, he will do what the courts refuse to do. He will give back to her life! He'll restore to her what has been taken. Jesus comes today into your life and into your family saying, "Get up, get out of your low self-esteem! Get up out of your self-hatred! Get up out of your confusion! Get up out of your pain! Get up out of your loveless life! You are somebody special to me, and in my eyes you are loved and you are lovable."

Tamar doesn't have to cry anymore. She can start singing with Jairus's daughter, "Blessed assurance, Jesus is mine! O what a foretaste of glory divine! Heir of salvation, purchased of God, born of His Spirit, washed in His blood. This is my story, this is my song, Praising my Savior all the day long!"

The Reverend Robina M. Winbush

AN EASTER PRAYER

When I'm down and out
Plagued with doubt
—Reassure me, Lord.

When I'm "fired-up" feeling mean,
Needing to blow off a little steam
—Calm me, Lord.

When those whom you sent me to serve
Give me grief I don't deserve
—Uphold me, Lord.

O God, give me an overcoming Spirit.

When my words or actions are not true
My heart distraught because I've failed you
—Forgive me, Lord.

When my body is in disrepair
And I think no one cares
—Restore me, Lord.

When pain strikes that I can't describe
Prevailing, no matter what the doctor prescribes
—Heal me, Lord.

O God, give me a triumphant spirit.

When the financial stress overwhelms me
Burdens so great I cannot see
—Provide for me, Lord.

A loved one is lost and I'm filled with sorrow
Feeling unable to face tomorrow
—Comfort me, Lord.

As I walk life's road day by day
Never knowing what will come my way
—Prepare me, Lord.

O God, give me a victorious spirit.

When evening shadows finally descend
As I approach my life's end
—Receive me, Lord.

When I enter Your Holy Presence
Praise and Joy shall be my essence
—Thank you, Lord.

My Resurrection and Life!
Amen.

The Reverend Marinda Harris

CERTAIN WOMEN—WITHOUT FEAR OR TREPIDATION

AS CHRISTIAN WOMEN TODAY, we cannot be who we are nor do what we do without some realization of the importance of women of the Bible. However, not to be ignored is this question raised by Dr. Meyers: "Would or should women today want to emulate their Israelite forebears?" From what we know, women of ancient times had little or no equality when it came to their male counterparts. Is this lack of egalitarianism something to long for or to envy? Or is it the source by which we gain greater insight into our accountability for relationships regardless of race, sex, gender, or national origin? Granted the Bible is male-oriented. It has been a male-oriented world for generations. Why even in Norfolk, Virginia, it was illegal for women to wear corsets in public until the law was changed in 1906! In every instance and through all circumstances, it is important for us as women to receive the messages of our forebears and move our own lives forward. We are to do so without fear or trepidation, for you see, biblical messages, all the stories of the histories of races and women and men, transcend all time and space.

Life-changing experiences can make us one of two things—wimps or heroines! Life-changing experiences can make us do one of two things—fold or stay in the game! The choices are ours. This was the case of the unnamed woman who found herself as the uninvited dinner guest at Simon's house. Her life circumstances heretofore played like "Another World." She was said to be a woman of sin, a woman who sold her body for the pleasures of men, a prostitute. None of us can be exactly sure how this woman ended up as she did, but we can safely assume that she had no one to care for her. She perhaps had no marketable skills that would make her employable. Perhaps all the male members of her family had died and she was without any family member, unlike Ruth and Naomi. Perhaps she had known despicable hunger and did whatever she could to get food to quiet the hunger pangs in her stomach. Maybe this unnamed woman longed for compassion and desired to be treated like a human being. Maybe she "hired" herself out just so she could hear the sound of someone else's voice, or have the touch of another human being. Whatever the reasons for her existence, it was at Simon's home that she became prominent. She placed herself in a position where who she was could no longer be ignored or dismissed.

Being in Jesus' presence had to be a life-changing experience for this woman. Why else would she behave as she did? Without fear or trepidation, she washed Jesus' feet with tears of both sorrow for her life and joy for just being in his presence. Without fear or trepidation, she extended to him the kiss that welcomes strangers. Without fear or trepidation, she anointed his feet with precious oils. Jesus, in turn, affirmed the woman's faith, forgave her sins, and offered her peace. But the unnamed woman had a price to pay for the free gifts given to her by Jesus. She had to move forward without fear or trepidation. She was no longer relegated to live on the fringes of society supported by dysfunctional institutions. She instead needed to find her way to a community that acknowledged celebration for sins forgiven. This unnamed woman needed to find a welcoming family that would care for her and nurture her newfound faith. She must have affirmed for her the kind of unconditional love that was given her by Jesus, the kind of love that keeps forever open the doors of forgiveness. The unnamed woman is a role model for us because of her lack of fear and trepidation.

Just as Luke told us the story of the unnamed woman, he tells the story of certain other women whose lives were also changed. These certain women had been restored to health of mind, body, and spirit by their belief in God and Jesus Christ. These were women who were included in and joined with others in Jesus' ministry. We know their names. Among them were Mary called Magdalene; Susanna and Joanna, the wife of Chuza, one of Herod's stewards. As Chuza's wife, Joanna could have easily relied on her husband's position to establish her own standing in the community. She instead joined the ranks of women like Lydia, a successful businesswoman who specialized in purple dyes. These women used their abundant resources to help finance Jesus' ministry. These were women of "independent means."

In the total scheme of things, we have composites of certain women who were from various economic backgrounds—those who were wealthy and among the socially acceptable and the economically comfortable. There were those who were of modest means and those who were destitute, poor, and homeless. The common link between them all was that these certain women had their lives changed by some aspect of Jesus' ministry. Fortunately for us, they moved forward without fear or trepidation. The list does not end with Joanna, Susanna, and Mary Magdalene. The list includes certain women like Claudia, Euodia, Syntyche, Dorcas, and Acadia. They were certain women who committed themselves to a vision of a new kingdom and a new way of living.

The list of women goes beyond those whose stories are told in the Bible. We know about Harriet Tubman, Sojourner Truth, Amanda Berry Smith, Frances Ellen Watkins Harper, Ellen Craft, Silvia Dubois, Eleanor Eldridge, Lucy Craft Laney, Ida Wells-Barnett, Charlotte Forten Grimké, and Anna Julia Cooper. The list goes on and on. To be women and to be alive is a God-given privilege! We know the stories of our mothers, grandmothers, great-grandmothers, aunts, sisters, cousins! We remember with pride the names of women who made their contributions as certain women, and we are grateful for their faithfulness. Like certain other women, they did not rely on "former things of old, but prepared themselves to accept the new things" of life in Christ Jesus. They, like their predecessors, were the "good news women" who were dedicated in their service, vigilant in their zeal for life in their churches, their communities, ardent in their compassion for others, passionate for the gospel, and faithful to their insights into God's Word made incarnate through Jesus Christ. Tens of thousands of other certain women willingly respond and make self-commitments to service in the kingdom present here on earth. These certain women are to be recognized for their efforts and their responses to duty.

We celebrate the twenty-fifth anniversary of African American Presbyterian clergywomen at a time when our nation and the world are in turmoil. We celebrate these certain women when we are called on to remember the cost of discipleship. As certain women ourselves, have we reconnected with the responsibilities of intensive training in discipleship? Do we have attitudes that acknowledge the demands, the powers, and the dangers of being servants of God? Are we aware of the challenges around us that call on us to do public teaching which takes place at meals, where we educate each other about table fellowship, where we teach one another the real meaning of community? Do we acknowledge our fears and make vows to overcome them? As religious leaders who celebrate the mission and ministries of the saints who have journeyed before us, do we turn up our noses at those women who happen to be unwed mothers, drug abusers, alcoholics, or prostitutes? Do we who celebrate Presbyterian African American clergywomen challenge our own prejudiced behavior and attitudes because other men and women do not have jobs like we do, shop at the same stores, or bank at the same bank? Do we accept and make space for the uninvited? How do we respond to those whose skin color is different from our own, or whose language is foreign?

Our faith, our religious values, are pivotal to us in every aspect of our lives. We have heard again a call to action, for we are members of the eternally divine kinship. We are free and emancipated. We can wear corsets in public! There were certain women who were our role models. They were women who served their communities and their churches without fear or trepidation.

The Reverend Opal Gurlivious Smith

A PASTORAL PRAYER FOR CONVOCATION SERVICE

O GRACIOUS AND EVER-LIVING GOD, we come this hour to this appointed place with deep yearning to be your faithful people and with a deep desire to encounter you at the edge and at the center of human experiences.

God, we come before you grateful for your love—not understanding it, but holding fast to it. We are awed that you love us when we do not at times either love ourselves or one another. We are awed that you love us not only in our pain, not only in our rejoicing, but you love us even in our bumbling confusion.

We pause to say thank-you. We thank you, God, that you claim us and know all things good for us and that you are working in our lives to strengthen and guide us as we begin a new academic year.

We praise you for opportunities to serve in your kingdom as pastors and teachers, as parents and students, as support staff and administrators, and as members of the board of trustees. May the work we do glorify you and serve your purpose in making this community and this world a good home for all your people.

We praise you for you Holy Spirit—transforming us, challenging us, and empowering us to live a life worthy of your calling.

God, we give thanks for the support and encouragement we receive from others—our families, friends, and colleagues; for the dedication and diligent work by our students, faculty, staff, administrators, and board members.

We give thanks for the mission of your church throughout the world and for special theological institutions and colleges.

Merciful God, hear us now as we pray for humankind.

We pray for those who are sick in mind, body, and spirit or circumstance.

Bring hope to those whose lives are filled with despair and calm our seniors as they prepare for exams and the call process. Give confidence and assurance to those among us who make new beginnings.

God, be present with the lonely and forgotten. Comfort those who are grieving the loss of loved ones and loss of relationships. Bless those suffering from the devastation of natural disasters.

We pray, God, that you lead all nations in the way of peace and justice. Guide those who are in positions of leadership that they may rule justly. Be with the President of the United States, the Cabinet, and the Congress as they make crucial decisions that affect not only our lives, but also affect the lives of your people throughout the world.

Grant us the ability to find joy and strength, not in the strident call to arms, but in stretching out our arms to embrace our brothers and sisters in the striving for peace and justice for your love's sake.

We pray for ourselves that as people created in your image, we will be true reflections of your justice and mercy, and your truth that makes each of us free. Focus us and make us whole, and grant us the discipline and courage to commit ourselves to visionary, convincing, and bold Christian leadership and service in your church in your world. We offer this prayer in the precious name of Jesus Christ our Savior. Amen.

DO WHAT YOU HAVE THE POWER TO DO

MARK 14:3–9 RECORDS THE STORY of Jesus' anointing at Bethany by the woman with an alabaster jar filled with costly ointment. When the disciples harshly criticized and berated her, Jesus said to them, "She has done what was in her power to do."

As an African American clergywoman, I am drawn to this biblical story often, for it invites every woman today and every Christian person to do just that: Do what you have the power to do. Here is my paraphrased version of a portion of the biblical story. This unnamed sister crashes the dinner party at Simon's (the leper) pad. Her presence at the meal does not even faze those eating dinner. She charges forth and things begin to happen. She breaks open the alabaster jar of precious perfumed oil and pours the whole thing on the head of Jesus—no dabs! We are talking about "Georgio" price tag! No cheap stuff! The sister moves right into action, anointing Jesus even before asking. The disciples gathered there become livid! How dare she waste this expensive perfume! They retort, "Why, she could have sold that perfume for a fortune and given the money to the poor! It is almost one year's salary for workers!" By now Jesus has had enough! "How dare you bother this woman; leave her alone. Go chill out! She has done what was in her power to do."

According to biblical writers on this text, women in the culture of first-century Jerusalem were denied public witness and voice, and were condemned to silence in the company of men because of tradition. But this unnamed, unwanted, excluded, invisible, voiceless woman dared to deal with life as she found it—just as we African American clergywomen struggle with life in ministry today.

As we stand at the beginning of the twenty-first century, some old patterns and traditions are being renegotiated. How all this is played out and renegotiated on the world stage and lived out in the community of faith will be determined to some extent by people's willingness to meet on common ground around human issues that hold us captive—such as sexism, racism, classism, ageism, homophobia—the list is endless. How we as clergywomen negotiate and renegotiate our relationship in this ministry partnership might well be determined by how anchored and ordered we are in God's Word, how secure we are in sharing leadership and power, and how clear our vision of mission is for God's church.

I am intrigued by how little is known about the woman in this anointing story, yet, what impact her presence and witness had among the dinner guests. Who was this woman? She was one who knew Jesus for herself and acted accordingly; she had a personal relationship with Jesus. It was faith, not her fear, that caused her to take on the established order, for she clearly understood what it meant to say, "If God is for you, who can be against you?" She was a silent proclaimer of the truth, where the designated disciples failed to "hear" and "listen." They seemed confused about Jesus' purpose and mission. Jesus had told them on three different occasions that he would suffer and die. They thought they had it made—suffering and cross-bearing and death surely could not be a part of the equation for discipleship. They became anxious and they argued about who would be given the best place of honor. This woman, through her decisive and powerful action and without saying one word, shouted to the world a message that is still remembered: "This is the Anointed One!" This is the Messiah, the long-awaited Savior of Israel."

Perhaps each of us today as African American clergywomen can relate in some way to this story. For through this woman's faith and by her action she embodies those qualities of love, generosity, and courage that are in part the liberating good news message of the gospel, which we also are to proclaim to the whole world. She showed faith discipleship.

Sister sojourners in ministry, I offer these three qualities—love, courage, and generosity—for us to embrace as we continue to do ministry with God's people.

- Love—On a daily basis, we surely must order our steps in God's Word of love as we go forth to do what we have the power to do with God's people. Love will strengthen us to be able to avoid all forms of unfaithfulness. The prophet Isaiah reminds us, the Lord says: "I have called you by name, you are mine. You are precious in my eyes and honored. And I love you!" *Dare to love!*

- Courage—Dare to have courage to denounce oppression and injustice. Whenever and wherever we see injustice and abuse, confront it. Go forth and triumph, my dear sisters in Christ, for we have been liberated with an awesome Holy Spirit as God's daughters. God, through Jesus Christ's life, death, and resurrection, has already taken the first step for us. And we, surrounded by a great cloud of witnesses, *dare* to have courage to be who God has called us to be at such a time as this.

- Generosity—Each one of us has our own alabaster jar filled with precious gifts. *Break open your alabaster jar!* Your gift of power is what you give to the world in service to others. The world awaits us! *Dare* to show generosity.

How dare you . . . How dare she—do what you have the power to do—break open your alabaster jar. Your gift of power is what you give to the world in service to others.

The Reverend Ernestine Blackmon Cole

QUIET TIME WITH THE LORD

I have often stopped to wonder
Why am I always in a hurry?
Can I make it through the daylight
without some fuss and worry.

When the night has come upon me,
And I take time to settle down,
I hurry to my sacred space
and the quiet nighttime sound.

There is something about that quietness
that brings me face to face
with all my daily failures
that confront me in that space.

But, oh, the peace and joy
as I talk with God alone.
Not bothered by the chatter
or the ringing of the phone.

It is in that sacred space
that peace and joy abide.
All of life's encounters
temporarily tossed aside.

Now, when the day is over
and my day's work is done,
I hurry to that sacred place
to meet God's only Son.

Then it dawns upon me,
Striking a very familiar cord.
I am in a hurry
to spend quiet time with the Lord.

The Reverend Dr. Arlene W. Gordon

GOD STORY

And this is for
colored women preachers
who have considered divinity
clinging to hospital railings
whispering hope in the ears of young
sistahs drinking kitchen products
climbing sheer inclines of treachery
with no safety procedures outlined
to climb in the windy and ponderous
pulpits of dying churches
to proclaim a living and righteous gospel
with death-defying feats
making brick with no straw
saving the babies like Shiprah and Puah/Hebrew Midwives
one name meaning mouth,
the other meaning handsome.
And this is for
colored women preachers
still climbing Leah's ladder
unwanted and unloved
but fertile as all the fragrant valleys that
cradle civilization and life
springs and wells and plays
in our libation poured out
lips.
We tell God's story
again and again.

THE BRONX I

Muggers, poets, and lovers
saints in fur collars
church lady hats and funeral parlor fans
old Scottish hymns
people my journey
down Public School 26 long green
hallways corridors where

immigrant ships never sailed
and slave knowledge curdled self-love.

In church they let us sing new songs with new
Converse sneakers
and loved us in cookies and juice and pencil-sharpening service
with flannel-board stories and faithful hugs and
story Bibles to hug and read.
God remembered the scared and lonely little boy all alone
Samuel
like
me.

Muggers, poets, and lovers
caress my journey
through tropical homes on opposite hemispheres
with buried ancestors
floating Middle Passage
gone
and new diaspora dreaming haunting
Dream book numbers and
odd ancestral rules.

Muggers, poets, and lovers taunt
Babylonian exiles the best and the brightest
taken from homelands to the Ivy League
whispering rocking transportation
on elevated train platforms sniffing cuchifritas
to sherry slipping cliffie hanging.

Letting down rap-un-zel
dreaming in Ivy tower
Letting down my nappy hair and
x-scaping to

Muggers, poets, and lovers
Fragments in the heart of God-story/Unfolding.

The Reverend Rose Eileen Niles McCray

WE COME IN HEARTFELT PRAYER: A LITANY

Leader: God of grace and compassion, we come to dedicate these hearts to you. Hearts that contain our sincere prayers for others. We seek your intervention in our lives, in the events in which we find ourselves, and in the circumstances that are beyond our control.

People: We come in heartfelt prayer.

Leader: The world outside is busy. Everywhere, there are sights and sounds of people starting a new day. But we are here: and we thank you for this place of worship that brings us rest and reflection.

People: We come in heartfelt prayer.

Leader: It is here in this community that we feel the sorrows of the world and look forward to the opportunities awaiting us. But we know from the messages written on these hearts that outside people are searching for food, seeking a job, looking for a place to sleep.

People: For them we come in heartfelt prayer.

Leader: Loving God, our concerns are for people in prison, people in exile, people suffering in every imaginable way. There are families in distress and people who will not make it through the day without another drink or a pill.

People: Merciful God, we lift them up to you in heartfelt prayer.

Leader: We pray for those who suffer from debilitating diseases. Give them courage to hold on to the goodness of life, even in the face of despair. We also pray for those who seek healing from broken relationships. Give strength to those who have gone through the anguish of divorce and other conflicts of relationships.

People: Because we carry them in our hearts, we come in heartfelt prayer.

Leader: O God of compassion, let us feel the strength and energy that flows from this worship service, and let this spiritual force transform not only our lives but the world around us. Let us also be your instruments of mercy and love.

People: As we come in heartfelt prayer, we live in the assurance that nothing will ever defeat us, so long as we hold the Christ within our hearts. We now go forward from this day with perseverance and hope, knowing that your goodness and grace will fulfill our every need. Amen.

The Reverend Rhoda C. Nixon

ACCORDING TO GRACE AND POWER

IN EPHESIANS 3:7–10, the apostle Paul writes:

> Of this gospel I have become a servant according to the gifts of God's
> grace that was given to me by the working of his power. Although I
> am the very least of all the saints, this grace was given to me to bring
> the Gentiles the news of the boundless riches of Christ, and to make
> everyone see what is the plan of the mystery hidden for ages in God
> who created all things; so that through the church the wisdom of God
> in its rich variety might now be made known to the rulers and
> authorities in the heavenly places.

Paul writes to the church at Ephesus a word of encouragement
even as he is in the midst of pain and physical imprisonment. But this
gospel given to him "according to the gift of God," not human beings,
must be preached at all cost. When God calls one into service, there is
to be a compelling urgency to be obedient. Surrendering one's life
sincerely for the sake of the gospel is not necessarily an easy road for
anyone—woman or man. But we are "entrusted with a commission"
(1 Cor. 9:17), and "woe to [us] if [we] do not proclaim the gospel!" (1
Cor. 9:16b).

To my sisters in the gospel, in spite of everything, in spite of
obstacles that seek to imprison the messenger, and sometimes the
message, whether it be physical, cultural, institutional, or anything
else, we must preach the Word. Preach the Word of the One who has
called us according to his gift of grace and power. This amazing "God
who created all things; so that through the church the wisdom of God
in its rich variety might now be made known" (Eph. 3:9–10)—this God
makes no mistakes! This assurance gives me boldness and humility to
share the good news with a world in need of redemption. For the voice
of God called my name, and I won't turn back; I can't turn back.

The Reverend Doris Glaspy

PRAYER OF CONFESSION

MOST MERCIFUL AND EVER-PRESENT GOD, we, your people of African descent, humbly bow before your throne of grace, confessing to you, O God, that we've not always been proud of our African heritage. We confess that we have not been obedient to your holy word that instructs us to teach our children and our children's children the truth of our history. We confess, dear God, that not only have we not embraced our heritage, but there have been times in our lives when we've looked at ourselves and thought we were less because of our history. Forgive us, Lord God, that we've been so limited in our understanding of who we are and who you truly are. A God who never makes a mistake or creates junk. You've been with us all the days of our creation.

We now confess that when the thorns bore deep and the blood ran red, you were there with us, holding us in the bosom of your arms. We confess all our sins as we now endeavor to honor you as we honor ourselves being made in your image on this day.

In the precious name of Jesus, the Christ, we pray. Amen.

The Reverend Gwendolyn Deloris Magby

GHANA: REFLECTIONS OF THE MOTHERLAND

IN JANUARY 1994, I was blessed with the opportunity to visit the Motherland: Ghana, West Africa. A party of seven seminary students led by a professor and his wife spent three weeks visiting Presbyterian congregations in Ghana. During my last days at Trinity College, an interdenominational seminary in Accra, Philip Mintah, one of the first-year students, asked me: "What stands out most about your time in Ghana?" I thought for a few moments and then said to him, "How familiar it feels being here."

The weather was hot and humid like July and August are here. The landscape of Ghana reminded me of Virginia. The mountains on the way to Abetifi and Ho reminded me of the mountains on the way to Charlottesville. As we rode toward the coast to see the slave castle at Elmina, the land was reminiscent of Tidewater and Hampton Roads, where I lived as a child. I listened to the surf, walked the beach, and stuck my feet in the waters of the Atlantic just like I have done on many occasions at Virginia Beach. It is estimated that 30 million of West Africa's strongest were captured and held in castles like Elmina during the African Holocaust. It is estimated that 10 million survived the ninety-day horror of the Middle Passage.

There are familiar expressions of faith.

I was awakened every morning at Trinity by the sounds of prayer groups singing hymns and praises. As I listened to them, I remembered a story my father would tell of falling asleep listening to the church choir practice downstairs in the living room of his home.

The constant awareness of God's power was expressed in prayers: prayers for traveling mercies, a good night's sleep, for making the smallest decision, for just being there through the day. In conversation the awareness of God and God's presence was very natural and easy. Three-fourths of the worship service was corporate worship: singing praises, singing confessions, singing thanksgiving, singing supplications, singing their theology, and making their faith a part of their lives. Christ brought the message of hope: redemption, transformation, healing, renewing, overcoming, victory, and returning. Their lives reflect their message. Christ is culture in Ghana. Hope sustains Ghana.

When I returned to Richmond, the oppressive and pessimistic mood of this culture was jolting. I acutely sensed rage, frustration, helplessness, and hopelessness. Words like crisis, victim, abuse, crime, and violence leapt out of conversations, music, literature, and legislation. Abuse by individuals, policies and procedures, systems, and structures were, and still are, being meted out in the name of love, peace, and justice. Initially I resisted, but slowly I could hear myself voicing some of those same words of hopelessness and powerlessness. I would cringe when I realized what I had done, and then say a quick prayer asking God to redeem the words.

Now that I have had the opportunity to step outside this culture, the phrase "Keep hope alive" has taken on a new meaning and urgency. To keep hope alive is to speak that which is unseen as if it were. To keep hope alive is to live the gospel of Jesus Christ and take the risks, make the sacrifices, and accept the consequences of being an agent of change—of transformation.

PRAYERS OF THE PEOPLE

WE HAVE ENTERED YOUR HOUSE, O Lord, weary from working for your kingdom all week. We come this morning not only to worship but to be cleansed; to have the stain of our sins removed by the power of your blood; to be rinsed with the clear, sparkling, living water of your word and dried with the breath of the Holy Spirit.

We come so that we can be equipped to work for your kingdom, made spotless by the power of your blood, refreshed by the rinsing of your word and the sweet fragrance of the Holy Spirit.

O Lord, we bring our cares and concerns to you. We pray for all who are struggling with the trials and tribulations of life. Be with us, Lord, lift our spirits, and give us that peace that transcends all understanding.

We pray for those who are sick, those who are in hospitals, those in nursing homes, and those who have no home. We pray for those who are in prisons and jails, not only those that have steel doors and iron bars but those prisons of aching bodies, paralyzed bodies, tormented minds, and numbed memories. Help us to meet their needs by the guidance of the Holy Spirit.

We pray a special prayer for our city, our state, and our nation. We pray for our leaders; guide them in their plans for the future. Give them the wisdom and the strength to do the right things and make the right decisions.

We pray for ourselves, that we move in the faith you have given us, that we see with your spiritual eyes and listen to your voice. Give us the strength of your Holy Spirit in our inner being so that Jesus can dwell in our hearts.

We ask in the name of Jesus the Christ, who taught us to pray.

PRAYER OF ILLUMINATION

NOW LORD, prepare us to hear, see, and be nourished by your word. Break up the hard crust of our intellect, weed out the thorns in our spirits, and remove the stones from our emotions so we can be rich fertile soil that hears and understands your word. Pour the living water of your Holy Spirit on us so we can produce a crop of good works one hundredfold. Amen.

The Reverend Paula Owens Parker

TO WHOM DO WE BELONG?

The next day John again was standing with two disciples, and as he watched Jesus walk by, he exclaimed, "Look, here is the Lamb of God!" The two disciples heard him say this, and they followed Jesus.

(John 1:35–37)

IF YOU WERE TO DIE TODAY, what would your obituary say? Would you be linked to a community or an organization? Would the most important items be where you worked, where you lived, or what church connections you had? Would the newspaper list whom you were married to, what family you were from, or what city you came from? Would it list how much you owned or what you possessed? *To whom do we belong?*

If Channel 2 decided to do an in-depth interview on your life as a special-interest story, what would people say? What would your next-door neighbor say? What would your doorman say? Would you be defined as a good Presbyterian, a faithful Christian, an asset to the community and to the church? *To whom do we belong?*

We belong to God. And our God is a God who is present and active within the whole creation. So who are we? We are Christians, followers of Christ, who is the light of the world, the author of peace and concord. We are a community that bears witness to the light and to the glorious hope found in Jesus Christ our Lord.

To whom do we belong? We belong to Christ. We are Christians seeking to discern God's will for our lives. We are Christians seeking to live faithfully as Jesus did, to serve the common good, to bind up the brokenhearted, and to care for those who are lonely. We want to touch and be touched by the "Lamb of God, who takes away the sins of the world."

Prayer: Grant us, O God, a mind to meditate on you, eyes to behold you, ears to listen for your word, a heart to love you, and a life to proclaim you. Through the power of the Spirit of Jesus Christ our Lord. Amen.

The Reverend Rhashell D. Hunter

PITHY REFLECTION

THE CALL TO THE MINISTRY OF WORD AND SACRAMENT led me to the discovery of the sacred space of church within the walls of academia. My work as an academician fulfills the role of servanthood as I engage in the sacred commission of teaching and mentoring men and women as they prepare for their role in the church and nontraditional places of ministry.

While my call is to New York Theological Seminary, I have the blessing of being part of the ministerial staff of First Presbyterian Church of Mt. Vernon, New York, where I serve as the Parish Associate. I am blessed to serve with another sister, the Rev. Rose Niles McCrary, who is an anointed, appointed, and adorned leader of the congregation as well as in the community.

My work with Sister Rose has confirmed my belief that women can have a common vision and work together for the good of the kingdom. However, many of us have been co-opted, confined, and colonized so long that we need one another to help lead and provide loving, liberating support. To this end, I seek to be part of the cosmic call to work toward the healing and wholeness of women. A people are only as strong as their women. Unity through love!

The Reverend Eleanor Moody-Shepherd

A MINISTRY OF FIRSTS

I AM A THIRD-GENERATION PRESBYTERIAN, reared in the Greenfield Presbyterian Church in Waterford, Mississippi—a church my grandfather, Jacob "Dock" Curry (born 1885), helped to organize. I have had the privilege of being the first Presbyterian woman from Waterford, Mississippi, to be ordained to the ministry of Word and Sacrament, the first Presbyterian woman from Marshall County, Mississippi, to enter the ministry, the first African American woman ordained by St. Andrew Presbytery, and the first Presbyterian woman of color to be ordained to the ministry in the state of Mississippi.

The Reverend Belinda M. Curry

A TRIBUTE TO HAGAR'S DAUGHTERS

I CAN IDENTIFY with the rejection of Hagar's experience. In October 1997, while on a trip to Ethiopia with several African American clergy, I came face to face with how deep the divide is between African and African American women and men. The group arrived at the ancient city of Axum, home of the Queen of Sheba and her palace and the home to a temple that Ethiopians believe to contain the original Ten Commandments, given as a gift to the Queen of Sheba by King Solomon. The Ethiopian Orthodox Church, however, forbids women to enter this particular temple. I was shocked when my clergy brothers who marched with us against racism and against Jim Crow segregation and who cried with us at the "door of no return" at such slave castles as Elmina in Ghana, deserted us, betrayed us, forgot us, broke covenant with us, and left us outside of the temple doors. While I respect the culture and tradition of the Ethiopian Church, the nature of my Reformed theology teaches me that Jesus and the truth transcends culture. That my clergy brothers from various denominations were not sensitive and did not opt to stand with us, that they willfully participated in ecclesiastical and cultural segregation, was appalling. I would like to salute Dave Wallace, dean of Johnson C. Smith Seminary, the only male who had the courage to stand with the clergywomen of various faiths to include the Rev. Dr. Katie Cannon. This experience has been relived on numerous occasions by sisters who have been baptized into sorrow, birthed into a culture of neglect and jealousy.

Ours is a daily struggle for recognition to find our voice in a society that continues to struggle with our title as reverend and refuses to hear the good news which we were born to proclaim. When confronted with this reality I turn to the comforting and liberating Word of God. I look to my biblical ancestors who made it through the wind and the rain— biblical characters such as Hagar, an Egyptian slave of Sarah and Abraham.

In Genesis, we read that the son born to Hagar and Abraham provoked rage in Sarah, to which Abraham acquiesced, resulting in the exile of Hagar and her son, Ishmael. For Sarah it was an issue of jealousy. For Abraham it was an issue of cowardness. For Hagar it became an issue of survival, life, and destiny. Hagar the survivor, who was rejected by her contemporaries, forgotten by biblical scholars, overlooked and unappreciated by women who bore the same struggle, not only survived but became the mother, leader, queen, and nurturer that God had ordained her to be. Because of her survival and great legacy, she is my "shero."

Hagar's story parallels the story of countless African American clergywomen who have also given up the first fruits of their loins and the essence of their souls. Clergywomen have been misidentified as the backbone but never the breastbone; always raising the money to build the new church but never to stand behind its pulpit; ordained by the people as good enough to be associate pastors but not senior pastors; and called to nurture the children in church school but not to be the spiritual leaders of the whole body of Christ.

Clergywomen once ordained are invited to the table only to be later rejected by the body they are called to serve. Women who share their gifts in the church have them trivialized in public spectacle in the name of the Lord. Hagar's story is our story—we share a common pain, common experience, and common destiny, which makes us daughters in the tradition of Hagar.

I am personally and professionally drawn to the story of Hagar, so much so that I refer to all the children of my ministry as Hagar's children and all women of African descent as Hagar's daughters. I work in the urban inner city of Baltimore, where over 70 percent of the children in my ministry are from single-parent households. The outreach ministry of the church where I labor is made up of women between the ages of eighteen and thirty-five—women trying to make ends meet, keep food on the table, clothes on the backs of their children, and money in their pockets; women who have babies to satisfy uncommitted absentee fathers, many of whom believe their manhood is defined by their ability to produce a child but haven't the faintest clue what it takes to love and raise a child. I refer to all these women as Hagar's daughters—who have to pick up the pieces and work out a plan of survival for themselves and their children. Hagar's daughters, like Hagar herself, will make it through.

Their children, like Ishmael, are born into a world filled with chaos, and suffer at the hands of racism, classism, and sexism. These children, Hagar's children, are affected by the concrete ceilings that stop their mothers from advancing in this global economy. Children, Hagar's children, are born into a relationship in which poverty is a constant companion, share the same mother but not the same father, change residency and schools as often as they have birthdays. These children, Hagar's children, wander around in the urban desert of our inner cities without a permanent address or a place to call home. These children, Hagar's children, whose mothers sometimes are incapable of mothering, are passed from person to person or have been rescued by grandparents or family members.

Hagar was a woman who survived the odds. She was a slave with an oppressed identity. However, even with these external limitations, God saved her. God turned her burdens into blessings and her trials into triumphs and her heartaches into hallelujahs. When Hagar was vulnerable, victimized, weak, and about to surrender, God saved her, made her strong, and used her in God's salvation story. God offered Hagar a new world, a new life, and another chance for her and Ishmael, a world and life dependent on God and God alone. With God on her side she was able to survive and to thrive. God in God's wisdom chose the unlikely, the oppressed, the disenfranchised, the hardworking, God chose the woman who had no land, no promise, no money, no man, no future, no property, and no church and made her the queen mother of an African nation. Hagar, sent into the desert to die, will never be forgotten.

I see myself as a proud daughter of Hagar. Just as God called Hagar from the desert into the promised land, God also calls Hagar's ordained daughters from the red hills of Georgia, the crowded streets of Baltimore, the sandy beaches of California, the mountains of Colorado, the plains of Kansas, and the hills of North Carolina. God reaches out, resurrects, and empowers us to rename ourselves, to claim our identify, and to take our rightful place.

God destroys the concrete and stained-glass ceiling for Hagar's daughters and children, and we rise like the phoenix from the ashes. We rise to liberate the body that has oppressed us, the women who have rejected us, the men who have not fully supported us, and the institutional church that has not advocated for us. So, we—180 of Hagar's African American Presbyterian ordained daughters—rise, armed with love, courage, faith, endurance, perseverance, vision, knowledge, and power to lead all God's people from the wilderness into the promised land.

The Reverend Karen V. Brown

PRESBYTERY CHARGE

(Given at my ordination by my brother, the Reverend Jimmie Hawkins)
You are facing a quadruple jeopardy in that, you are a *female* living in a male-dominated society, an *African American* female in a society that puts women on the bottom of the pay scale, a *Presbyterian* female seeking ordination in a denomination that ordains females but does not necessarily push to place those females in the parish, and an *African American* Presbyterian female in a denomination that is struggling to be inclusive of all races in the midst of diversity. Realize your obstacles and stand firm in your faith.

FAVORITE QUOTES

Being of one body yet sharing many voices is the daily life and strength of black women.

(Julia A. Boyd)

We need to dig and jump into the land we come from; one woman after another, one dream upon the other, calling up who we are.

(Ntozake Shange)

I WONDER

WHEN I AM IN THE MALL, watching people walk around me, many times I look at their expressions and I wonder what's in their hearts. I wonder if they know Christ. I wonder if they have what they need in order to live a healthy and whole life. I wonder if they are happy with life. I wonder if they have the peace they need in order to function in their different environments. I wonder all these things because I know that what we need to endure life is on the inside of us. It is what's on the inside that enables us to endure. It is what's on the inside that empowers us as we deal with life issues. It's what in our hearts that indicates if we truly have a relationship with God. It's what is on the inside that God is concerned about, for what is in our hearts motivates our thoughts and our actions.

Over the centuries, we African American females have a history full of women who have challenged the dilemma of being born into a gender class that deals with racist, sexist, and classist mentalities. Our contributions in all areas of life (literacy, scientific, academic, psychological, and so forth) have been ignored and devalued, and the task is left to the black female to lift up our contributions to American society. We can look throughout our history and see that God has raised up and continues to bring forth many great African American female leaders in all arenas of life—from Cleopatra to Phyllis Wheatley, to Mae Jemison, to Mary McLeod Bethune, to Marian Wright Edelman.

The Reverend Annie Vanessa Hawkins

A CALL TO WORSHIP

(for the children's sermon)
Come, children, come!
Receive the inheritance that has been promised to you for generations.
Listen now to the words that will give you strength;
hold close the teachings that will give you power.
Walk now in the wisdom of the Spirit;
Spirit wants to dance with you,
Spirit wants to search you and prepare you for . . .
God has chosen *you* to help the people cross over into the promised land.

A CALL TO ACTIVE WORSHIP

When I think about the goodness of Jesus and all that he's done for me,
my soul cries out Hallelujah!
But that is not enough!
I must not be content with joyful cries and expressions of praise and
    adoration.
God expects my praise and adoration along with some type of
    demonstration that I have
internalized the change that has resulted from my understanding of
    how good God is.
If my praise doesn't translate into spiritual octane that compels me to
    take risks for the
liberation of oppressed people, then I am just making noise, and God
    already has too many
part-time noisy lovers.
The hour is upon us where those who worship God must worship in
    Spirit and truth!

ODE TO THE QUEEN SISTER WHO IS ABSENT FROM HER PRESENCE

Hey sis, why are you walking with your heels twisted over like that?
You gonna ruin the souls of your feet.
You can't reclaim your queendom through a pipe or his pleasure.
You can't build black children wearing a worn-out soul.
You better find yourself a good pair of shoes to wear.
Here you are, wear mine, 'til you find a pair that fits.

THE WOMEN WHO FOLLOW JESUS

Some of us must be willing to die so that others of us can live.
Some of us must be willing to live so that others of us can die.

Some of us must be willing to be well while others of us heal.
Some of us must be willing to have courage until others of us find strength.

Some of us must be willing to teach so that others of us can learn.
Some of us must be willing to learn so that others of us can teach.

Some of us must be willing to study so that others of us can know truth.
Some of us must be willing to exercise knowledge until others of us find wisdom.

Some of us must be willing to stand so that others of us can sit down.
Some of us must be willing to sit down so that others of us can stand.

Some of us must be willing to be silent so that others of us can speak.
Some of us must be willing to be peacemakers while others of us come to terms with power.

Some of us must be willing to sing so that others of us can dance.
Some of us must be willing to dance so that others of us can sing.

Some of us must be willing to have hope while others of us have faith.
Some of us must be willing to be childless so that others of us can know mothering.

Some of us must be willing to lead so that others of us find direction.
Some of us must be willing to seek direction so that others of us can lead.

Some of us must be willing to receive vision while others of us reclaim our sight.
Some of us must be willing to demonstrate love while others of us work through our pain.

Some of us must be willing to be wives so that others of us can
remain single.
Some of us must be willing to be single so that others of us can be
wives.

All of us must be willing to understand that none of us can be all
that she is called to be, unless each of us is willing to know the
otherness of this journey.

The Reverend Stephany D. Graham

I "CAN DO"

I can do all things through him who strengthens me.

(Phil. 4:13)

THIS IS A PERSONAL STATEMENT. "I" pertains to me. This means that I can exchange my self-confidence for faith in Jesus Christ. To make this statement one must have a personal relationship with God, and that is what Christianity is, a personal relationship with God.

This means that I am able to do what I ought to do if I trust God. Obviously there are some limits to what we can do, but I can do all things that are required of me.

> I *can* endure all trials and tribulations.
> I *can* perform all necessary duties.
> I *can* overcome conflicts.
> I *can* face every crisis.
> I *can* love even when it is difficult.
> I *can* forgive.

How . . . "in Christ." This is providential. What we do should be the things that concern Christ. Yes, he promised to give us the desires of our hearts, but our desires should be his desires. We must ask, Can Christ bless this? Is this the will of God?

The power of this message lies in "who strengthens me." Christ is the source of my strength. Christ, not I, makes all things possible. I must draw on this source. God knows what I need, and will give it to me as I need it, and when I am ready to receive it. We don't always get what we want when we want it, and maybe that is because we are not always ready for it when we want it, but God is an on-time God, and we must learn to wait on God.

So when in trouble, overwhelmed by life, burdened by commitment, staggered by requirements of service, torn with conflict, or facing crisis, remember, "I can do all things through him who strengthens me."

The Reverend Catherine M. Hughes

PRAYERS OFFERED AT INTERRELIGIOUS BRIEFING/CONSULTATION OF CONSCIENCE

MIGHTY GOD, the world is yours and the nations are your people. Take away our pride and bring to mind your goodness so that, living together in this land, we may enjoy your gifts and be thankful.

We come together to pray not just so that our own ideas will prevail, but we pray for the world you have created. We particularly offer prayers for this nation and for its elected officials.

We pray for policy-making centers where men and women talk together and work together in legislative bodies, assembly sessions, and United Nations gatherings.

We also pray for the policy-making centers in our own systems—our presbyteries, dioceses, conferences, and synods. We pray that these centers of ecclesiastical decision making stay truthful to your call for justice, and freedom, and fairness, for all your children. Give them strength, dear God.

We pray for the modern-day prophets among us who speak out, sometimes risking reputation and friendship.

We offer our prayers for the silent faithful people among us, asking that they may be given the courage to speak out against injustice.

Oh God, your justice is like a rock. Your mercy is like pure flowing water. If we have turned from you, judge us and forgive us—then give us the wisdom to turn back to your way, for without you we are a lost people.

Lead us from public deceptions that weaken trust;

Lead us from divisions among us based on class, race, gender, or sexuality;

Lead us from wealth that will not share;

Lead us from poverty that feeds on bitterness; God lead us!

God, lead our political officials from overlooking the hurt, the imprisoned, and the needy among us;

God, lead our political officials from a lack of concern for other lands and peoples.

Lead them from narrowness of national purpose and from failure to welcome the peace you promise on earth.

Eternal God, before you nations rise and fall; before you nations will grow strong or they will wither according to your design.

Help us to overcome our country's wrongs and to choose your paths in reunion and renewal.

Give us a glimpse of the holy city you are bringing to earth, where death and pain and crying will be no more, and nations will gather in the light of your presence.

Talk sense to us, God, talk sense to us, so that we may talk sense to those who are elected to lead our nation.

Knowing that there is no law or liberty apart from you, let us serve you modestly, as devoted people. We pray these things in the name of the one God of us all. Amen.*

The Reverend Elenora Giddings Ivory

*Adapted from *The Worshipbook*, pp. 127–129. Copyright © 1972 The Westminster Press. Used with permission.

SOMETHING DRAWING ME ON

She opened the door of her apartment, glad to finally be home. The clutter was just as she had left it. It seemed to reflect the disorder in her life. Seminary studies were even more difficult than she had imagined. Her decision to quit an excellent job and return to school, especially seminary, took family and friends by surprise. In many ways it was a response to a life that had become void and unfulfilled, a passage point demanding a pivotal decision. Now, halfway through the curriculum, things were not any easier.

As she walked through the apartment, the level of clutter escalated. Evidence of the all-night, paper-writing marathon was everywhere. Pages of drafts, loose notes, open books, assorted dictionaries all demonstrated frantic, desperate attempts at writing. At least it was Friday.

She dropped the canvas bag of books she was carrying on the cluttered floor and dropped her purse on top of it. She tossed her coat on the back of a chair. In the bedroom, she kicked off her shoes and flung herself across the unmade bed. The late afternoon sun filled the room with a muted sadness. It fit her mood.

She allowed the exhaustion she had been fighting all week to take over her body. "God, it has been an awful week," she thought. She could not remember ever being this tired for this many days. She closed her eyes, pulled the covers over her head, sank into the pillow, and waited to die. Sleep, if not death, came easily.

When she opened her eyes again, the room was dark save for the haunting glow of a fluorescent streetlight. She felt herself emerging from a familiar place of deep sleep. She looked at the clock . . . 8:15 P.M. She had been asleep nearly four hours. Thoughts of unmet responsibilities immediately flooded her head and, within seconds, made a knot in her stomach. She stretched, closed her eyes again, and contemplated whether to lie still and gently succumb to the sluggishness that beckoned her back to sleep or force herself to a decidedly more unpleasant "awakening."

Without looking, she stretched out one hand, found the radio, and turned it on. The distinctive sounds of a flute drifted softly into the room. A melodious jazz arrangement of a familiar African American slave song lured her toward another level of consciousness. The words to the song came to mind: "Lord, how come me here? I wish I never was born. They sold my children away, Lord. I wish I never was born." The sounds of the flute were so beautiful, so haunting, so powerful.

The melody fed her mood, and she did not want it to end. Finally, she forced herself to get up; a hot shower and shampoo would certainly help. As the hot water ran over her hair and body, the song echoed in her head: "Lord, how come me here?" That really was the question. Granted, there was a world of difference between the tortuous grief of an African American slave mother and her own self-imposed, stress of graduate studies. Yet, the slave mother was part of her legacy. Despite profound circumstantial differences, this was still *the* question. "Lord, how come me here?"

Why was she pursuing a seminary degree and ordination? The psychological stress, physical exhaustion, spiritual doubting, financial indebtedness, job uncertainties, high academic standards, isolation from old and trusted friends—everything seemed to leave her physically, intellectually, and spiritually bankrupt. Yet, she knew she had the skills for ministry and believed in the power of the Christian church to bring sanity to the world. She still believed the Presbyterian Church was the right place for her and that seminary training was critical for the kind of leadership role she hoped to assume in the church. Besides, so much was already invested; quitting did not seem a viable option.

Still, where would she get the energy to keep going? Such secular and faith dissonance had become as exhausting as any of the more practical problems. The repeated conflict in her own mind was creating a depression that had become a constant companion. She sang the words aloud: "I wish I never was born." She did not really mean it, but still . . .

Clean clothes and clean hair made her feel a little better. The song was still with her. There was a cassette somewhere among her things. Searching through her tapes, she picked up one she had not listened to in a long time. She put it on the player and found the song she wanted. The powerful a cappella voices of five African American women floated out and began to fill the void in her spirit. Their voices harmonized and created amazing sounds, each voice becoming a distinct, musical instrument.

I feel something drawing me. I feel it pulling and urging.
I feel something drawing me on.
There is something so divine, down in this heart of mine.
I feel something drawing me on.

The voices were earthy and guttural, deep with passion and commitment. She turned off the lights and, sitting in a rocking chair, listened to the song again. The movement of the chair kept rhythm with the voices, and the sounds filled her and truly touched deep within her. The tape ended and clicked itself off. She continued to rock softly, thinking of old and new friends, old and new places, old and new commitments.

Finally, she stood and surveyed the bedlam. Slowly, deliberately, she began tossing useless papers into the trash, closing books and returning them to the shelves. She needed to clear up this mess. There was a lot of reading to do, and other class projects needed attention. She sang quietly as she worked, "I feel something drawing me on."

The Reverend Meri-Li Douglas

Listing of African American Clergywomen by Ordination Date

1974
Katie Geneva Cannon
Jacqueline Alexander

1976
Elenora Giddings Ivory
Joan M. Martin
Dorothy F. Cross
Devia Pellam Phinisee

1977
Gloria J. Tate

1978
Rita L. Dixon
Marsha Snulligan Haney

1980
Amitiyah Elayne Hyman
Portia Turner Williamson
Winona Jones Ducille
Morrisine Flennaugh Mutshi
Bernice Warren
Phyllis M. Felton
Ophelia Manney (deceased)

1981
Alma W. O'Bryant
Frances Camille Williams-Neal
Bernardine Grant McRipley

1982
Dorothy Wright
Rosalind Y. Powell

1983
Patricia Mason
Deborah Mullen
Clarice J. Martin
Myrtle McCall
Brenda D. Brooks

1984
Venetta D. Baker
Yvette L. Dalton
Beverly S. Bullock
Barbara Ndovie
Willie M. Brazil

1985
Kathryn Smallwood
Toby Gillespie-Mobley
Jacqueline Blackstone
Delrio Ligons-Berry
Nancy Thornton McKenzie

1986
Retha Mungin-Nelson
Joanne E.Brown

1987
Grace Bowen
Wanda Lundy
Janice Nessibou
Louwanda Harris
Gail Nelson
Diane Givens-Moffett

1988
Pauline R. Haynes
Brenda B. Tapia
Diane Corrothers Smalley
Julia Prince
Sandra K. Edwards

1989
Karen Pearson
Robina M. Winbush
Patsy Nichols Redwood
Mary Newbern-Williams
Carmen Mason-Brown
Karen Bellin
Jacqueline E. Taylor

Jon-Irma Burkette
Marinda Harris

1990
Opal Gurlivious Smith
Virginia M. Brown
Emma Thompson
Carieta Cain-Grizzell

1991
Ernestine Blackmon Cole
Arlene W. Gordon
Tanya Wade
?Rose Eileen Niles McCrary
Sylvia J. Wilson
Rhoda C. Nixon

1992
Jaqueline Tillman
Ella Busby
Ida M. Wooden

1993
Lillian Anthony
Floreta Watkins
Gloria Johnson
Doris Glaspy
Sylvia T. Walker
Ira Wooden

1994
Karen V. Brown
Paula Owens Parker
Ethelyn R. Taylor
Gwendolyn Delores Magby

1995
Vanessa Mills
Rhashell D. Hunter
Jeanne Daniels
Valeria Harvell
Diane Winley
Vanessa Knight
Alyce Kelly

1996
Muriel Burrow
Angela B. Archer
Sandra Heeb

Alika Galloway
Iris Tucker-Lloyd
Patrice Nelson
Eleanor Moody-Shepherd
Veronica Goines
Sandra Jorden

1997
Gay Lynne Byron
Belinda M. Curry

1998
Nina Bryant
Annie Vanessa Hawkins
Stephany D. Graham
Agnes Blackmon
Gloria Bolden
Troy Janel Dixon
Cynthia Williams
Catherine Hughes
Meri-Li Douglas
Andrea M. Rodgers

1999
Patricia Bacon
Audrey Deas
Yvonne Pendleron
Jane Johnson
Jermaine McKinley
Kikanza Nuri-Robins
2000
Evangeline Taylor
Minette Hope
Dorcas Miller
Brenda Mosley-Moore

Date of Ordination Not Known
Georgiama Keegle
Addie Peterson
Doris Peterson
Julia Robinson
Joan Salmon-Campbell
Jean Watlen
Ida Wells (honorably retired)

Index of
Participants and Contributors